Log Cabin

REDISCOVERED BY MACHINE

Brenda Brayfield

American Quilter's Society

P. O. Box 3290 • Paducah, KY 42002-3290
e-mail: info@AQSquilt.com

Located in Paducah, Kentucky, the American Quilter's Society (AQS) is dedicated to promoting the accomplishments of today's quilters. Through its publications and events, AQS strives to honor today's quilt-makers and their work and to inspire future creativity and innovation in quiltmaking.

EDITOR: BARBARA SMITH
GRAPHIC DESIGN: ELAINE WILSON
COVER DESIGN: MICHAEL BUCKINGHAM
PHOTOGRAPHY: CHARLES R. LYNCH

Library of Congress Cataloging-in-Publication Data
Brayfield, Brenda.
    Log cabin rediscovered by machine / by Brenda Brayfield.
      p. cm.
    1. Machine quilting--Patterns. 2. Patchwork--Patterns. 3. Log cabin
    quilts. I. Title.
    TT835.B665 2001
    746.46'041--dc21
                    2001000910

Additional copies of this book may be ordered from the American Quilter's Society, PO Box 3290, Paducah, KY 42002-3290, or online at www.AQSquilt.com.

Dedication

This book is dedicated to my husband, Roger, who makes everything possible. I am grateful every day for your love, support, and encouragement in all that I do.

MOUNTAIN RETREAT, 54" x 54". Designed by Brenda Brayfield, pieced by Sabina Granbois, machine quilted by Carol Seeley.

Acknowledgments

Many people contributed to the creation of this book, each in his or her own special way. I am truly grateful for their help, support, and encouragement.

To my sons, Jim, Ryan, and Kevin, for their patience throughout the years as Mom explored a variety of creative endeavors.

To my "daughter," Brenda, for appreciating the joys of quilting.

To my mother, Maureen Clough, for always believing in me and encouraging me to follow my dreams.

To Barbara, Linda, and Bob Marr of Wineberry Fabrics, Surrey, British Columbia, Canada, for everything you did to make that dream a reality.

To Donna Mercer, my first quilting teacher, for sparking a flame that is still burning bright.

To my good friends, Theresa Bakos, Jean Chisholm, and Sabina Granbois, who were my "firm foundations" as I was writing this book. Since the inception of this project, their input and assistance have been invaluable.

To Carol Seeley of Campbell River, British Columbia, for reserving time in her very busy schedule to do the machine quilting for me. Carol, the quilting is magnificent!

To the quiltmakers who gave so generously of their time, their talent, and their wonderful quilts.

To my students, whose positive feedback and enjoyment of the technique inspired me to draft more blocks and ultimately write this book.

To Penny McMorris, who has been so helpful and supportive.

To Dixie Haywood for information provided on top-pressed foundation piecing.

To everyone who asked, "How is the book coming?" Your interest was a constant source of motivation.

To my editor, Barbara Smith, and the talented team of experts at the American Quilter's Society. I am honored to be a member of the AQS family.

My heartfelt thanks to all of you. Your contributions made this book a reality.

Contents

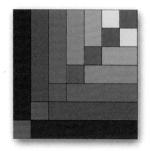

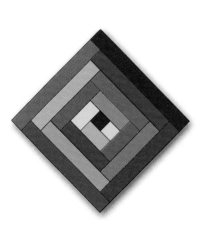

Introduction

A simple 7" Log Cabin block was the ember that sparked the inspiration for this book. It was a class sample for a workshop I would be teaching. The quilt was made of 35 – 7" Log Cabin blocks. Each block had 17 logs, and the strips were cut 1¼" wide.

Fabric placement was random, so cutting the logs to size was not practical. I opted for the cut-as-you-sew method of construction. Halfway through the first block, I realized that an accurate, consistent block would be an unrealistic expectation for any new quilters in the class. Too many logs, too many seams, and too much margin for error.

The logical solution was foundation piecing. Admittedly not an enthusiast for foundation paper piecing, I always manage to cut the fabric piece too small, then overcompensate by cutting the next piece too large. Then I am annoyed with myself for wasting fabric, not to mention having a stiff neck and tired arms from holding the block up to a light source.

In the true spirit of quilting, I quickly drafted a foundation block on the computer and, within minutes, was back at the sewing machine. With renewed enthusiasm and a revised attitude, I set out to make my first foundation block.

I got as far as the third log. In turning the block over to admire my work, I discovered the edge of the strip was caught in the seam. That was all the encouragement needed – into the bin it went!

Foundation piecing was the way to proceed, but I wanted to sew on fabric, not paper. But from the fabric side, I would not be able to see the stitching lines because they would be on the bottom. What would happen if I turned the block over and sewed with the lines on top? No, that wouldn't work either. The fabric would cover the lines. Well, where is it written that the lines have to be stitching lines? Why can't they be fabric placement lines? I can sew a ¼" seam without having a line. And so it began.

Back to the computer and the drawing board. I knew what was wanted and needed, and I was amazed and delighted to be able to achieve it. It was almost too good to be true. I had drafted a foundation that was easy to sew, fun to use, and one that would produce perfect blocks every time. As a real bonus, I was able to sew on the fabric. What more could anyone want? The technique was an instant success with my students. They loved the ease of construction and the accuracy of the blocks.

Given that my quilting career began in 1993, it is understandable that the only method of foundation piecing I was familiar with was the technique in which the fabric is placed on the unmarked side of the paper and the sewing is done on the marked side. I have since learned that the technique I "discovered" is a traditional method and a favorite of several professional quilters.

Modern duplicating procedures and computer software have made it possible for me to give this method of foundation piecing a re-birth. It is my pleasure to introduce you to an old friend. I am confident that once you try this technique, you will be delighted to have made the acquaintance.

In This Book

It is my objective to provide you with an easy, accurate technique for making Log Cabin blocks, accompanied by a variety of design possibilities. This book is based on a foundation technique called "on-top" or "top-pressed" piecing. The lines on the block are fabric placement lines, not stitching lines. You sew with the fabric on top and the paper on the bottom. I recommend starting with a traditional Log Cabin block to learn the basic technique. Once you are familiar with the fundamentals of construction and trimming, then proceed to the blocks with angled logs.

Please take the time to read through the directions specific to each block or technique. You will find the tips especially helpful. Consider this your Log Cabin workbook. In it, you have all the tools and tips of the trade to build your Log Cabins. Choose from a wide variety of blocks in sizes ranging from 2¾" to 7" to design an original quilt or use the blocks in a favorite commercial pattern. Whichever road you take, I am confident you will find a block within these pages to meet your needs.

Enjoy the journey!

Chapter 1

Getting Started

Tools and Equipment

Having the right tools and equipment will increase your enjoyment of quilting. Purchase the best equipment you can afford. Your quilts are worth it.

Rotary cutter

The rotary cutter is an indispensable tool that allows you to cut accurate strips in record time. I can't imagine making a Log Cabin quilt without one. There are a variety of models and sizes available, and there are even ergonomically correct cutters. Select the size and style that feels the most comfortable in your hand. The 45mm cutter is the most popular size, and my personal favorite. There are yards of strips to cut in a Log Cabin quilt. A sharp blade will reduce wrist and arm fatigue. Always have a spare blade on hand, just in case a wayward pin finds its way onto the cutting mat.

Cutting mat

In addition to the rotary cutter, you will also need a good quality, self-healing rotary cutting mat. The smallest size to purchase is 18" x 24". This size will accommodate the folded width of the fabric.

Rulers

You will need a 6" x 24" clear acrylic ruler to cut the strips. A 9½" square ruler is also useful for squaring the fabric and trimming the blocks to size. Gripper dots placed on the underside of the 9½" square will prevent the ruler from shifting on the paper foundation.

Scissors

A pair of good quality scissors is a wise purchase and one you will never regret. I treated myself to a pair of 5" knife-edge scissors that are perfect for this technique. They are small enough to use at the machine for snipping threads and the ideal size for trimming fabric logs. In the cut-as-you-sew method, the rounded edge slides smoothly under the fabric strip without catching in the paper.

Thread

Use 50/3 all-cotton thread in a neutral color to match your lightest fabric. There are a lot of seams in a Log Cabin quilt, so buy a large spool or two. I make it a practice to fill five bobbins at a time. There is no good time to run out of bobbin thread, but the annoyance is lessened somewhat when a full bobbin is readily available.

Sewing machine

A well-maintained, straight-stitch machine with reverse stitch capabilities is all you need to successfully complete the blocks in this book. Reduce the stitch length to 16–18 stitches per inch or 1.5 for European machines. The smaller stitch perforates the paper and makes paper removal easier. It also helps to prevent loose bottom stitches when the paper is removed. Don't make the stitches too small just in case you have to "un-sew."

Balanced tension is important for good stitch quality. Do a stitch test with two layers of fabric on your foundation paper before making a block. Remove the paper and inspect the stitches. If the top thread is loose on the underside, increase the top tension.

Ideally, the foundation should be fully supported when you sew. If your machine does not have a portable slide-on extension table, you can use books to build up the area behind and beside your sewing machine.

Presser feet

The best choice is the walking foot. In this foundation technique, the fabric is on the top, the paper is on the bottom. The feed dogs cannot grip and move the paper as they do fabric. By using the walking foot, also called even-feed foot, there is one set of feed dogs in direct contact with the fabric.

Take the time to perfect a ¼" seam allowance by using your walking foot and you will produce accurate Log Cabin blocks. You cannot rely on the seam guides on the throat plate of the sewing machine, because they will be covered by the foundation block.

Present-day walking feet are marked with a ¼" seam guide. If yours isn't marked, fasten a small piece of white tape on the right toe. Place a piece of ¼" graph paper under the walking foot. Slowly lower the needle until it pierces one of the lines. Lower the walking foot. Use a fine-tipped pen to mark on the white tape where the ¼" graph line is in relation to the foot (Fig. 1–1).

The ¼" foot is also an option, but not one I recommend. This foot will give you an accurate seam allowance, but the fabric will not feed evenly under the presser foot. This is very noticeable on the longer logs. If uneven feeding is a problem, reduce the sewing speed, and when you notice the fabric beginning to twist, manually feed it under the presser foot with a sewing awl or other pointed object.

To compare the ¼" foot with the walking foot, cut four strips of fabric 2" x 6". Layer two strips and place them on a piece of white paper. With the paper on the bottom, use a walking foot and a ¼" seam allowance to join the two strips. Use a ¼" foot for the other two strips. Compare the two samples. Can you see and feel the difference? Log Cabin blocks with straight logs are forgiving if there is any variance in the seam allowance. However, blocks with angled units require greater accuracy.

Needles

For top foundation piecing, I prefer a #10 jeans/denim needle. It is a strong, sharp needle that produces perfect stitches top and bottom. Not all machines are the same. Experiment with different needle sizes until you find the one that is right for your machine. Purchase good quality needles.

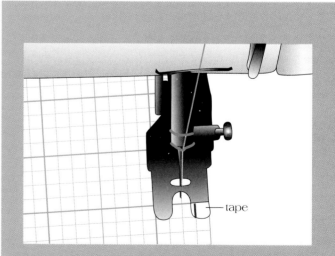

Fig. 1–1. Fasten tape to the presser foot and place ¼" graph paper under the foot. Draw a line on the tape at the ¼" mark.

The less expensive, lower quality needles will dull or break in no time.

Start with a new needle in the machine and be prepared to change it more often than you normally would. The paper will have the same effect on your needle as it does on your good fabric scissors.

Each time you change the needle, brush away the lint from the feed dogs and bobbin case. If you are able to remove the throat plate, do so, for a thorough cleaning. The tiny paper particles collect and produce more lint than regular sewing. It is important to change the needle regularly and keep the machine clean and lint-free.

Additional supplies
- Colored highlighter to mark outside logs
- Fabric glue stick
- Glass-head fine straight pins
- Iron and firm pressing surface
- Mechanical pencil for tracing the pattern
- Tracing paper
- Removable cellophane tape
- Fine-tipped black fabric pen, size .01 or .02
- Containers or boxes to hold fabric strips
- Pressing cloth for photocopied blocks
- 1" x 12" clear acrylic ruler
- Seam ripper (just in case)

Fabric Selection

Use 100-percent cotton fabrics and purchase the best quality you can afford. A little fabric goes a long way in a Log Cabin quilt. Indulge yourself and use fabric you really love. As you make more and more Log Cabin quilts, your eye will instinctively tell you which fabrics are good "loggers." You will automatically visualize entire bolts of fabric as narrow 1¼" strips.

Small- to medium-scale prints that contain only a few colors are the best choices for Log Cabin quilts. Select fabrics that have low contrast within the print as opposed to high contrast. Black and gray fabrics have low contrast. Black and white fabrics have high contrast.

Value refers to the apparent lightness or darkness of a fabric. The three main value groupings are light, medium, and dark, with varying degrees of value within each group. The contrast in value between fabrics can be strong or subtle, but for the design to be effective, it should be distinct. Value is relative. A medium fabric will read as light when placed next to a darker fabric. The same fabric will read as dark when placed with a lighter fabric.

It is important to vary the scale and texture of the prints you select. Mini florals, pin dots, and small gingham checks will look charming sitting on the counter at the quilt shop, but the finished quilt will lack interest. It will be a nice quilt, not a stunning one.

Large-scale, multi-colored prints tend to create confusion and disorder in an otherwise "tidy cabin." Often, the one color that attracted you to the bolt will be eliminated when the fabric is cut into narrow strips.

To get a better idea of what the fabrics will look like when cut into strips, stand the bolts in an upright row and view them from a distance. Is there enough contrast in value? Are any of the fabrics so close in value that one fabric blends into another? Ideally, each fabric should look distinctly different, but not so much so that it stands out from all the others.

Planned Log Cabin

In a planned Log Cabin quilt, the same fabric appears in the same log in every block. The most significant fabric in a planned Log Cabin is the outermost dark log. There will be more of this fabric than any other in the quilt. Be careful that this fabric is not so dark that it forms a secondary design of its own when the blocks are rotated and sewn together. To help keep this secondary design from forming, select two slightly different fabrics of similar value for the outside logs. Alternate their usage in the block construction and their placement in the quilt.

The center square should be a pleasing contrast to both the light and dark sides. If the center square is too light, the block will resemble a donut; if it's too dark it will resemble a bull's eye. Traditionally, each fabric in a planned Log Cabin block becomes progressively darker as you build toward the outside logs. When viewing a Log Cabin quilt, your eye automatically picks up the center square and then, log by log, moves to the outside.

In the quilt COUNTRY CHARM on page 47, the fabric values are staggered. Instead of the lightest fabric being next to the center, it is positioned between the medium and dark values. With shifted values, the block is no longer predictable. In addition to creating visual movement and interest, the value placement adds sparkle to the light logs, and the dark logs do not appear as heavy.

A planned Log Cabin is a great first quilt for the beginning quilter. It is very doable and certainly not as overwhelming as a multi-fabric quilt. I limited myself to eight fabrics in COUNTRY CHARM to demonstrate that attractive quilts can be made from a limited palette. The theme, or border, fabric was chosen first, and then seven other fabrics were selected to support it. The center square, inside border, and binding are made from the same fabric.

Log Cabin quilts that have a single fabric for all the light logs are visually pleasing, especially when the design includes appliqué. The fabric in the logs does not compete with the appliqué design. It enhances it.

Multi-fabric quilt

A multi-fabric quilt with random placement is my personal favorite. My blueprint for building a scrappy Log Cabin is to decide on the color combination first, then visit every quilt shop in the area, and proceed to purchase a quarter yard of everything in my color palette. It's a license to buy fabric.

Inspiration for the color palette can come from a variety of sources: your stash, a theme fabric, or a photo in a quilt book or magazine.

This is the perfect opportunity to get out of your safety zone by challenging yourself to select a "non-favorite" color combination.

You can select tone-on-tone fabrics and fabrics that contain two or more of the colors in the theme print. Two-color fabrics are useful and effective in Log Cabin blocks. In addition to bridging two fabrics, they also lead you to the next fabric choice.

Previewing fabrics

To preview your fabrics, cut one inside log from all the fabrics you plan to use. Place all the strips on a design wall and then step back to view them. Suspend strips over the edge of the ironing board if you do not have a design wall. This will serve the same purpose. Does the "zinger" fabric now appear zany? Does any one fabric stick out like a sore thumb? Before eliminating this fabric, try moving it. Possibly the rogue strip just needs a new neighbor.

To confirm your fabric choices before beginning to sew, prepare a mock-up block. Trim the seam allowances from the center square and logs. Glue the logs on a foundation block, and you will see exactly how the finished block will look. Trim the paper at the fabric edge and place the "finished" block on your design wall to critique.

> **TIP:** Use the fabric edge of the previous fabric log as a placement guide, not the line on the foundation.

Keeping track

When making a multi-fabric quilt, it is useful to prepare a legend of all your fabrics. To make a legend, cut a 2" length from each strip and glue the lengths on a piece of lightweight cardboard. I find it is easier to look at the fabric legend than to sort through the strips in a container. The legend is also used to take "roll call" at the start of a new sewing day – a checklist to make sure every strip is present and accounted for. It's also a good idea to make a purse-sized legend to carry with you for impromptu fabric-shopping.

The first three or four blocks in a multi-fabric quilt will take the longest. Once you become familiar with your fabrics, the block construction will go much more quickly. You will know instinctively which fabric you need without having to audition a variety of fabrics.

With a multi-fabric or scrap quilt, you will undoubtedly include a fabric that, in the final analysis, just doesn't work. Eliminate the fabric, but not the completed block. It will only be in one, or possibly two, blocks, and it will go unnoticed in a large quilt. I strategically place these blocks near the outside edge or in the corners.

Modified planned Log Cabin

For this color recipe, select a common center and five or six lights and five or six darks. The fabrics should be similar, but not identical in value. Remember to vary the design, texture, and scale of the prints. Instead of using a different fabric in every log as you would in a multi-fabric or scrap quilt, use the same light or dark fabric for two consecutive logs. Vary the placement and fabric selection in each block.

In addition to being a lot of fun, this method makes an extremely attractive quilt. The varieties of fabrics used add interest and excitement to the quilt top. This recipe is also an excellent choice for the quilter who may be overwhelmed by purchasing the "right" fabrics for a multi-fabric quilt but who wants to break free of the structure of a planned Log Cabin.

Choosing border fabric

If the border is not part of the quilt design, it's a good idea to wait until the top has been completed before purchasing the border fabric. Often what you think is the perfect fabric turns out to be not-so-perfect after all. Fabric can assume a second identity when pieced with other fabrics. The quilt will tell you what it needs. Be prepared to listen to it. Remain open-minded and audition several different color choices. After selecting a border fabric, give it the 15-foot test. Are you still able to clearly distinguish each color in the print or do they blend together to form another less desirable color?

There are many border options to choose from, and many excellent books have been written on this subject. The most popular style is a simple one-piece border that showcases a theme or focal fabric. A narrow inner border in contrasting fabric will frame the quilt center and separate it from the outer border.

If possible, purchase sufficient fabric to cut the border on the lengthwise grain. A border cut on this grain will stretch less than one cut on the crosswise grain. If it is necessary to piece the border, remove the selvages and sew the strips together, end to end, with a straight seam and ⅜" seam allowance. Press the seam allowances open. When adding the border to the quilt top, offset a border seam and a quilt top seam. With the seams staggered, the border seam will be less noticeable.

Fabric Preparation

With the exception of fabric that is used for a baby quilt, I do not wash fabric; I soak it. For smaller pieces, a basin in the laundry room sink is adequate. I use lukewarm water and no additives. Place all like colors together, hand agitate, and allow them to soak for a few minutes, then tip the contents into the washer and spin dry to remove excess water. Do not wring the fabrics out by hand because this will set wrinkles that are difficult to remove, even with the most vigorous pressing. Larger pieces of fabric can be placed directly in the washer. Fill the tub with lukewarm water, select the rinse cycle and delicate setting, and agitate for five minutes before spin drying. Damp dry them in the clothes dryer.

Dark fabrics can be soaked individually to test for excessive color running. It is quite normal for some dark fabrics to release excess dye when first soaked. Don't be alarmed. Continue to rinse until the excess dye has been removed and the water runs clear. If the dye does not stop bleeding after repeated rinsing, do not use that fabric.

I suffer from mild allergies, so soaking fabrics first is not an option; it's a necessity. Soaking helps to remove the protective chemical coatings the manufacturers have used. If I work on new fabric, the heat from the iron releases the chemicals into the air, and I suffer…but I keep on sewing!

I prefer soaking to washing the fabric because I enjoy working on crisp fabric. In addition to retaining the as-new quality of my fabric, soaking also…

- removes any surface chemical residues,
- tests for excessive color running,
- shrinks the fabric,
- allows fabric to relax and return to the natural straight of grain.

To see the difference soaking or washing would make, square up the cutting side of a length of unwashed fabric by rotary cutting a narrow strip from the fold to the selvages. The cut should be perpendicular to the fold. Examine the threads at the cut to see how much off-grain the fabric is. Washing or soaking removes the sizing, allowing the fabric to relax and return to its natural straight of grain. Therefore your cut logs will be on grain.

I love steam for pressing, but my pieced blocks do not. I use steam for the initial pressing when the fabric is removed from the dryer but not for the sewing process. Pressing with steam puts moisture in the blocks, which may distort and shrink them. Even if the fabric is for a wallhanging, I recommend that you always wet it first.

To remove the excess water from smaller fabric pieces, I use a salad spinner. Works great! The only problem encountered so far is the occasional thread in the Caesar salad.

DESIGN WALL

A design wall is a worthwhile addition to any sewing room. It allows you to view the design from a distance and to observe how the fabrics relate to one another. Often, a fabric adopts a new identity when placed beside another fabric. What was blue can look green. What was bright can appear dull.

You get the truest picture of a quilt when it is viewed vertically. Stepping back from the quilt increases your range of vision, and you will be able to read the quilt as one complete unit, not just section by section.

There is always a work in progress on my design wall. The wall is particularly helpful if a fabric choice or design element is presenting a problem. It's beneficial to be able to walk away from the work and return later to view it with fresh eyes.

The design wall in my sewing room is used for every step of the quiltmaking process. Fabric selection, design choices, width of borders, and binding are always auditioned on the design wall before a final selection is made.

A portable design wall can be made from a piece of ceiling tile purchased at a building-supply store. Cover the ceiling tile with felt, thin cotton batting, or flannel. Your portable design wall can easily be stored behind a door or under the bed when not in use.

Work Area

Before beginning your next Log Cabin project, take a few minutes to organize your workspace into an L-shape, the most practical set-up for foundation piecing (Fig. 1–2). Simply place a table alongside you where you can reach it while seated at the sewing machine. In addition a side table creates a pressing area. An ironing board can serve as a temporary work station. Lower the ironing board until it is a comfortable working height.

You will need a firm surface for pressing. If the ironing board cover is too soft, the foundation block will sink into the pad when pressure is applied to the iron. In addition to creasing the paper foundation, it's difficult to get a sharp, flat seam when pressing on a soft surface. To create a firmer pressing surface, place a narrow board on top of the ironing board and cover the board with a folded bed sheet.

Fig. 1–2. This L-shaped work station, with a design wall on the left, provides maximum efficiency.

LOG CABIN REDISCOVERED BY MACHINE – Brenda Brayfield

Chapter 2
Foundation Piecing

Preparing Foundations

The accuracy of your finished blocks and quilts depends on the accuracy of the foundation copies. Taking the time to familiarize yourself with the different methods of reproduction will pay off with happy sewing and accurate blocks. You will need a separate foundation pattern for each block in your quilt.

Tracing

Tracing the blocks by hand can be time consuming, but if you need only a few blocks for your project, this is a simple, accurate method of reproducing the blocks.

Place a piece of tracing paper on top of the block pattern in the book and secure the paper with removable tape to prevent it from shifting as you trace. Use a mechanical pencil and ruler to draw the lines. In addition to the pattern lines, include the cutting extension lines, stitching guidelines, and log numbers.

Transfer pen

Transfer pens can be purchased at your local quilt or needlework shop. If the block you have selected is not symmetrical, you will need to make a mirror image of it before you can use the transfer pen. Trace the pattern lines, extension lines, and stitching guidelines on tracing paper. Omit the log numbers, unless you can write numbers backward. Turn the block tracing over and place it on a piece of plain white paper so you can easily see the traced lines through the tracing paper. Use a fine-tipped pen to retrace the lines on the tracing paper. Trace the mirror image on firm, white paper.

Refer to the manufacturer's directions for details specific to the transfer pen you have. Practice with the pen until you are able to achieve a consistent line width. Adjust the placement of the ruler on the block to accommodate the width of the transfer pen line. It is important to keep the lines as thin as possible because thick lines will alter the size of the block. After you have practiced, use the transfer pen to ink the lines on the pattern. This is your master pattern.

Use a dry iron to transfer the master pattern, image side down, to the foundation paper of your choice. The lighter the touch, the longer the master will last. Depending on how many blocks you need, it may be necessary to re-ink the lines when the image becomes faint. Write the log numbers on each block after it has been transferred, or keep the original pattern handy for quick reference.

Photocopying

The quickest and easiest method of reproducing the blocks is photocopying. There are some important things you should know about a photocopied block. There is the likelihood of distortion, and photocopy toner is water based and therefore not heat resistant. You cannot place a hot iron directly on a photocopied foundation block because it will smear.

Here are some tips for photocopying:

- Go to a professional copy center that will do the photocopying for you.
- Digital photocopiers produce the truest image with minimal distortion.
- Ask the operator to set the copy machine on "light" to reduce the amount of toner on the page.
- Bring a 9½" square ruler with you to test the accuracy of the block.
- Have one copy made, then measure the block in both directions to make sure they are the same length. When you are satisfied with the accuracy of the photocopied block, continue with the rest of the photocopying.
- Get all the photocopying done at one time, using the same machine.
- Make extra copies.
- Always photocopy from an original.
- When you are using a photocopied pattern, place a cotton press cloth on top of the block before pressing a seam.

Foundation papers

Log Cabin blocks with horizontal and vertical logs do not require a special foundation piecing paper. The foundation blocks I use are computer printed on 20-pound white paper, available in 500-sheet packages (ream) from any office supply store. The paper is inexpensive, holds the ink well, is easy to work on, and easy to remove. I use this paper because I prefer the stability of a firm foundation for lifting the block from the workstation to the sewing machine.

The weight of paper used by professional copy centers can be used for foundation piecing. Request a lightweight paper, which, fortunately, is usually the least expensive.

If you have purchased foundation paper before going to the copy center, ask if it is possible to use your paper in the copier. Some copy centers are hesitant to use paper that hasn't been designed specifically for their machines. The fiber content is unknown, and it might jam and damage their expensive machines.

There are many types of foundation papers available that have been designed especially for foundation piecing. One of the benefits of commercially produced foundation papers is the ease of removal. This is something to consider if there are a lot of small, angled pieces in the block. I used a commercial foundation for PINEAPPLE RHAPSODY on page 62.

It is not necessary to be able to see through the paper when using the top-pressed method of foundation piecing. Eliminating this criterion will give you more choices when you are selecting a foundation paper.

The most interesting thing I discovered while testing different types of foundation paper is that paper shrinks when a hot iron is applied to it. That had never occurred to me. I knew there had to be some explanation for why my blocks measured a perfect 7½" when printed, but when I went to trim the sewn blocks, the distance between the cutting extension lines was slightly smaller. Paper is a natural fiber, and it will *shrink* when heat is applied to it. The amount of shrinkage is directly related to how hot the iron is. Set your iron on the lowest setting that will allow you to press the seam effectively.

There are many types of foundation papers available on the market. We all have individual preferences. Some machines sew beautifully on one type of paper, but not as well on another. Be sure to take time to familiarize yourself with the available options and use the one that will work best for you and your machine.

Rotary Cutting

It's best to rinse, or wash, and iron fabrics before cutting them. Refer to Fabric Preparation on page 12 for complete details.

I find it awkward to align and cut strips from a large piece of fabric. Depending on the size of the piece, I will either remove one yard to work with at a time or cut the piece in half. I find these smaller sections are much more manageable.

To prepare your rinsed and pressed fabric for cutting, fold it in half lengthwise with wrong sides together. To align the selvages, place your index fingers between the two layers. Raise the fabric to eye level and shift the front layer between your thumbs and index fingers until it lies flat and wrinkle-free along the bottom folded edge (Fig. 2–1).

Place the fabric on a rotary cutting mat large enough to accommodate the folded width of fabric. The fold should be near the bottom of the mat.

Reverse the following cutting directions if you are left-handed. Square the left edge by aligning a square ruler, or other 4" to 6"-wide ruler, with the fold. Place a 6" x 24" acrylic ruler snugly against the left side of the smaller ruler (Fig. 2–2). Be sure the long ruler covers both layers of fabric. While holding the long ruler firmly in place, remove the square one. Cut from the fold to the selvage with a rotary cutter (Fig. 2–3). Continue to hold the ruler in position and slowly slide the fabric piece on the right away from the ruler. If you did not get a clean cut on your first effort, go back and re-cut any missed threads before moving the long ruler.

Fold the fabric in half again by bringing the bottom fold to the top selvages and aligning the just-cut side edges. You will be cutting through four layers of fabric (Fig. 2–4, page 18). To cut a 2" strip, place the 2" ruler mark on the just-cut fabric edge. The left side of the ruler will extend past the fabric onto the cutting mat (Fig. 2–5, page 18). Cut the strip from the fold to the selvage.

There is more likelihood of the cutting edge "wandering" when cutting through four layers, so

Fig. 2–1. Shift the top layer of fabric left or right until the fabric above the fold lies flat.

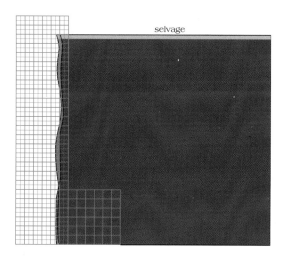

Fig. 2–2. Place the long ruler flush with the shorter ruler.

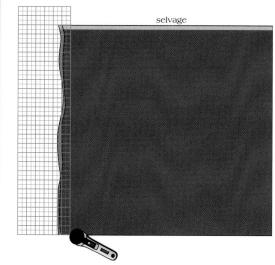

Fig. 2–3. Start your cut at the fold.

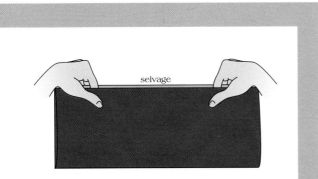

Fig. 2–4. Fold the fabric again, aligning the original fold with the selvages.

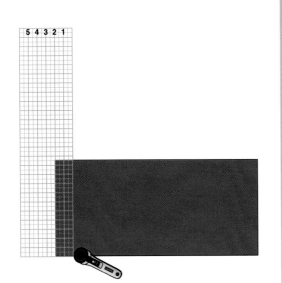

Fig. 2–5. Place the 2" line along the cut edge.

Fig. 2–6. Periodically check to see that your strips are straight when they are unfolded.

as you cut your strips, periodically, open one to check that it is still straight (Fig. 2–6). If the strip is crooked, unfold the fabric to two layers and re-square the cutting edge.

Log Cabin strips do not always have to be cut from the full width of the fabric. Any piece that can be cut to size for a log can be used. Fat-quarters, fat-eighths, and scraps are fine. If you have only a small amount of a favorite fabric, use it for the inside logs. Your piece will last longer and appear in more blocks.

Figure 2–7 shows the various parts of a typical Log Cabin foundation pattern. The capital letters correspond to the cut strip widths and relate to the letters in the pattern's cutting instructions. The numbers indicate the piecing order for the logs. The sequence for trimming the sewn block to size is also given on each pattern.

The lines on the block are fabric placement lines, not stitching lines. They must always be visible to ensure accuracy. To keep them visible, it is sometimes beneficial to cut scant strips. By cutting the strips scant, the log will lie just shy of the fabric placement line. Note, however, that cutting scant applies only to inside logs, not angled or outside logs.

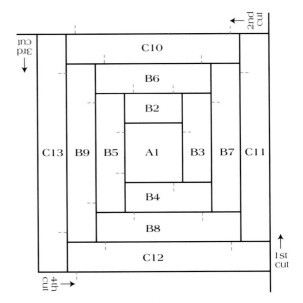

Fig. 2–7. Sample Log Cabin pattern.

The thickness of the lines on your ruler can affect your cutting. To ensure accuracy and produce scant strips, align the fabric edge with the leading edge of the ruler line, not the middle or the other side of it (Fig. 2–8).

Scrap Log Cabin

At the beginning of a new project, I place four empty storage containers beside my cutting table, one container for each type of log to be cut: light inside log strips; outside log strips; dark inside log strips; outside log strips. Never limiting myself to the required number of fabrics, the containers are usually full by the time I finish cutting one strip from each one!

When the wide strips are not long enough for an outside log, the extra width is trimmed off, and they are transferred to the inside-log container. When a fabric strip has been used up, a new strip is cut to replace it.

The word "generous" before a measurement means the log should be cut ¹⁄₁₆" wider than the measurement given. For a generous 1⅝" strip, position the fabric edge halfway between the ⅝" and the ¾" mark.

Planned Log Cabin

There are many ways to plan fabric placement for a Log Cabin quilt. In one traditional plan, pairs of consecutive logs are cut from the same fabric (Fig. 2–9). All the blocks are alike. One of the advantages of a planned Log Cabin is that the strips can be rotary cut into individual log lengths before you begin to sew. If you enjoy working from full strips, continue to do so. The finished block is the same whether the logs are "cut-as-you-sew" or pre-cut to size.

If you choose to pre-cut the logs, the strip widths are given in the pattern. To determine the length of each log, measure directly from the foundation pattern. For the inside logs, measure the distance between the two short sides. For the logs second and third from the last, add an extra ¼",

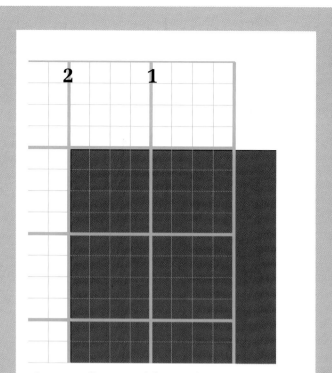

Fig. 2–8. Align your fabric with the leading edge of the line.

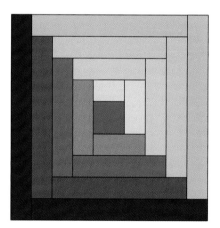

Fig. 2–9. In this block style, consecutive logs are cut from the same fabric.

> **TIP:** For a multi-fabric quilt, select a block whose center square and outside dark logs are cut the same width, or so similar that you could use the same strip for both.

and for the last log, add an extra ½" (Fig. 2–10). The extra lengths are needed because the outside logs are wider than the inside logs. This extra width ensures accuracy when trimming the block to size. Cut one piece of fabric for each log and make a sample block to test your measurements.

Now that you are sure of the measurements for pre-cutting your logs, unfold four strips of the same fabric. With the right sides facing up, layer the strips. If the strips are narrow, hot pressing the strips together will keep the stack neater for cutting.

Trim the selvages from one end of the layered strips. Starting from the trimmed end, cut the shorter log of each pair first, then the longer one. Continue cutting short and long logs along the full length of the strips. If you get near the end

TIP: With so many logs and so many measurements, here is an easy way to ensure that you do not cut the wrong fabric. Cut a small square of each fabric and glue the squares, in a vertical row, on a piece of lightweight cardboard. Write the cutting measurement beside each one. This vertical format will be easier to use than trying to "read" a Log Cabin block because we naturally read from top to bottom, not around in a circle. Leave this chart at your cutting station.

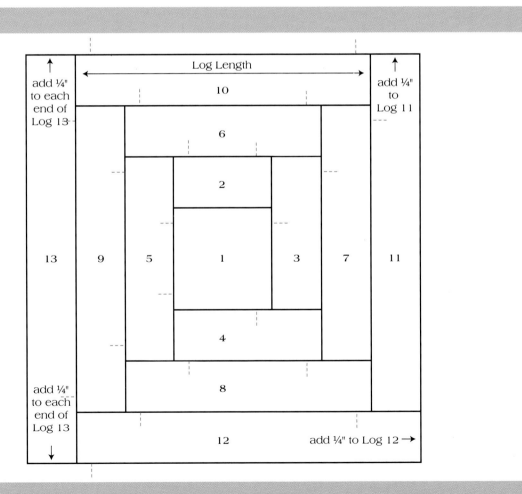

Fig. 2–10. For inside logs 1–10, measure from end to end (includes seam allowances). For outside logs 11 and 12, add ¼". For last log 13, add ½".

SAMPLE BLOCKS

When you make your sample block, ask yourself some questions. Do you like it? Does the small print read as a plain fabric now that it is cut into a narrow strip? Do you have enough contrast in value? Is your center square so dark that it resembles a bull's eye in the middle of the block? Does the zinger fabric you added for interest dominate the block? Is your outermost round of logs too dark?

These are questions you should answer before continuing to sew the remainder of the blocks. If you are not satisfied with the finished look of your first block, chances are you won't be happy with the next 35!

Sometimes, one block does not give a true indication of how the finished quilt will look. Make three more test blocks. Place the blocks on the design wall and view them with the light logs together, then view the blocks with the dark logs together.

Now is the time to make a change if you are not completely satisfied with your fabric choices. You have invested only one or two strips of each fabric and a little time. Being happy with your fabric choices, the completed blocks, and ultimately the finished quilt is the pay back on this investment. If you don't like one of the fabrics, the remaining piece is still large enough that it can easily be added to your stash for another project.

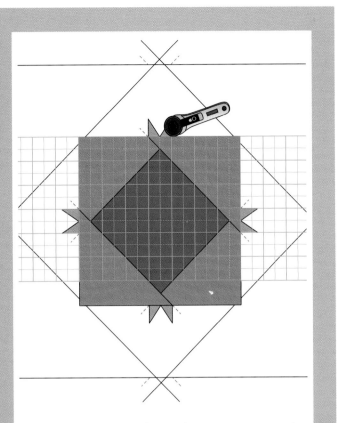

Fig. 2–11. Use a ruler and rotary cutter to trim the ears from on-point pieces.

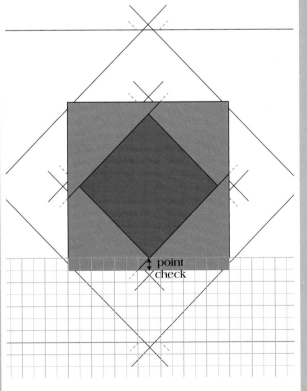

point check

Fig. 2–12. Place the ¼" mark on the fabric placement line for a point check.

and realize you cannot cut two logs from the remaining strip length, separate the layers and cut the shorter length from one pile and the longer length from the other.

Transfer the cut logs to an area adjacent to your sewing machine. Place the center square right side up and the logs face down, in the correct sewing order.

When strips are stacked and cut as one unit, the layers in the stacks may stick together. Fan the stacks first to separate the logs. Starting with the outside log, pick up one log from each stack and make a crisscross stack of the logs for one block in the palm of your hand. Finish with the center square. Now you are ready to make your block. It can't get any easier, or more convenient than this!

Block Construction
Useful terms

Here are some useful concepts and terms for constructing blocks:

Outermost log – The longest outside log. It is the last log added to the block, and it is the only log that can be turned back to reveal its entire seam.

Sew consecutively – Sew the first log, raise the needle and the presser foot, and without cutting the threads, rotate the block and sew the next log. Then clip the connecting top and bottom threads.

Ears – The portion of the seam allowances that extend past the fabric edge where two angled pieces are sewn together. The ears on Tulip Blocks can be trimmed during construction or when the block is completed and the paper removed (page 37). It's a good idea to trim the ears during construction for on-point blocks.

For accuracy and convenience, use your rotary cutting equipment. Align the ruler edge with the fabric placement line and, using the rotary cutter, trim the ears (Fig. 2–11). There will be a short cut in the foundation. This step serves three purposes: it removes the ears, the center part of the fabric placement line becomes visible, and the small cut in the foundation makes paper removal easier.

To avoid tearing the foundation block, do not make the cut longer than the width of the ears.

Pin down – Place a fine straight pin in the seam-allowance fold to keep a log flat. Pin into the fabric only, not the paper. Pin down half-square triangles, longer logs in regular Log Cabin blocks, and logs in Pineapple blocks that have been sewn consecutively.

Stitching guidelines – An accurate seam allowance and exact fabric placement are essential for on-point blocks. To assist you, stitching guidelines have been included in the patterns. The guidelines are ¼" from the fabric placement lines. Place the fabric edge on the fabric placement line, insert the needle into the stitching guideline, and lower the walking foot. Check the position of the edge of the walking foot in relation to the fabric edge and maintain this seam allowance as you sew to the opposite stitching guideline.

Point check – This is a simple procedure you can use to see whether a point will be lost when the next log is attached. Place the ¼" mark of a clear acrylic ruler on the fabric placement line. Do a point check to see where the point is in relation to the edge of the ruler. If the ruler covers any part of the point, the tip will be lost when the next log is added (Fig. 2–13).

If the point is covered, it also indicates that either the seam allowance or the fabric placement is not accurate, or possibly both. Check these before continuing with the remaining rounds. This problem will compound itself in an on-point block, and it is not self-correcting as in a traditional Log Cabin block.

If the point loss is significant, it's best to remove the triangle and try again. If the difference is minimal, only the width of a ruler line, simply draw a new stitching guideline. To do this, adjust the edge of the ruler until it rests on the point. In pencil, draw a new stitching line.

TIP: There are five layers of fabric at the point, and as careful as you are, the log may shift as it's being sewn. You may want to secure the log to the underlying point with a fine straight pin. Decrease the sewing speed as you approach the point.

Preparing to sew

Prepare to sew by setting up your sewing machine, as follows:

- Foot – Walking foot (dual-feed foot)
- Needle – 70/10 jeans/denim
- Thread – 100% cotton 50 weight
- Stitch length setting – 1.5 (16–18)
- Seam allowance – ¼"

TIP: Highlight the numbers on the four outside logs to remind you to change to a wider strip. If you are new to Log Cabin block construction, write directly on the foundation block, in pencil, which logs are light and which are dark.

Cut one strip from each fabric and make a test block. I can't stress this enough, especially in the blocks with half-square triangles. The cutting measurements provided are exact, but your interpretation of scant or generous may be different from mine. The objective is to have the sewn log finish just inside the fabric placement line.

In the block patterns, each log is identified with a capital letter and a number. The letter corresponds to the same letter in the cutting measurements and indicates the size to cut a strip or square. The numbers refer to piecing order.

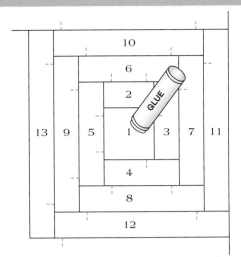

Fig. 2-13. Use a glue stick to hold the center fabric square in place.

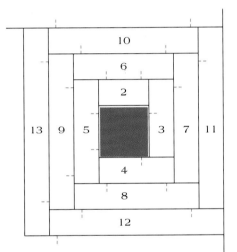

Fig. 2-14. Position the center square inside the lines.

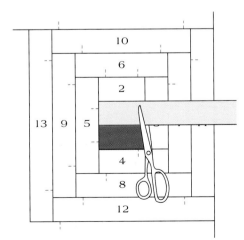

Fig. 2-15. With right sides together, trim the strip inside the line.

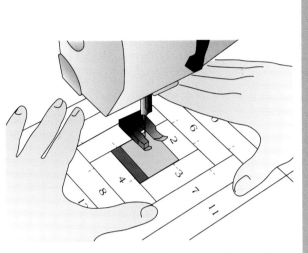

Fig. 2-16. Use your hands to guide the block as you stitch from fabric edge to fabric edge.

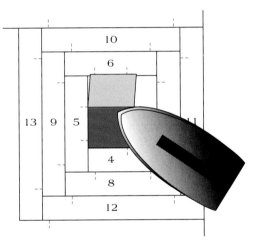

Fig. 2-17. With the side of the iron, press the logs away from the center.

FIRST CUT: Notice the cutting extension lines and the cutting order instructions on the pattern. Lay the block on your cutting mat with the edge marked "1st cut" positioned on the bottom right.

Align a 9½" square ruler with the cutting lines that extend beyond the top and bottom of the block on the right side (Fig. 2–20).

Make the first cut. Cut slowly. Remember, there is paper on the bottom, and it does not cling to the cutting mat the way fabric does. The block may shift if you go too fast.

SECOND CUT: Rotate the block a quarter-turn clockwise.

For blocks 6" and smaller, align a horizontal line on the ruler with the bottom edge of the block. Align the ruler's right edge with the top extension line (Fig. 2–21). Cut the second side.

For blocks 7" and larger, either pencil in an extension line or fold down the last log and use the side of the pattern as a ruler placement guide (Fig. 2–22). Cut the second side with the log folded. After making the cut, fold the log back to its original position before making the third cut.

THIRD CUT: Rotate the block a quarter turn clockwise. Align a horizontal line on the ruler with the bottom edge of the block. Measure from the left edge of the block to make the third cut (Fig. 2–23). For example, with a 6½" block (includes seam allowances), you would place the 6½" ruler line on the left edge of the block.

FOURTH CUT: Rotate the block a quarter-turn clockwise. Place the top edge of the ruler on the top edge of the block. Use the block's measurements to align the ruler with the bottom and left edges. For the example, you would align the ruler's horizontal and vertical 6½" lines with the bottom and left edges of the block. To make the final cut, start at the top edge and make a 1½" reverse cut. Return to the bottom edge and cut through to the top. You will feel when the two cuts merge (Fig. 2–24, page 29).

Consistent ruler placement and rotary cutting will produce outermost logs that are the same width. In the majority of Log Cabin settings, the

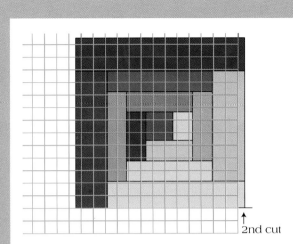

Fig. 2–21. Align the ruler with the bottom edge of the block and the top extension line to make the second cut.

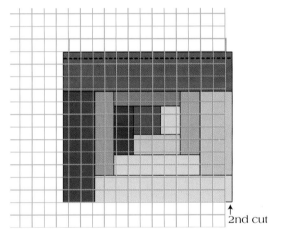

Fig. 2–22. Fold down the last log and use the side of the pattern to align the ruler.

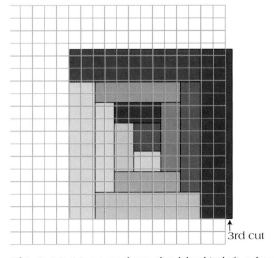

Fig. 2–23. Measure from the block's left edge to make the third cut.

SEAM ALLOWANCES

Seam allowances that are pressed in the opposite direction (opposing seams) are much easier to match than seam allowances that go in the same direction. Depending on the quilt setting, the outside seam allowances could end up going in the same direction when you join two blocks. When this happens, to ensure a perfect match, reverse the direction of one set of seam allowances. First, press the seam allowances flat, then press the allowances in the opposite direction, or with a toothpick, apply a small amount of fabric glue to one of the seam allowances. Accurately align the two seams and pinch the two blocks together. Pin as you normally would. The glue will secure the seam allowances and prevent the blocks from shifting as you sew.

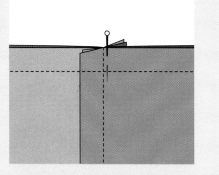

Opposing seam allowances are easy to match.

outermost log seams connect to form a straight line. If the connecting logs are different widths, the seams will be misaligned when two blocks are joins.

Removing paper

REGULAR LOG CABIN BLOCKS: The paper is removed before the blocks are sewn together. Paper removal in straight log blocks is easy. Start with the outermost log; pinch the outside seam at the top edge to prevent the stitches from raveling and, with the other hand, gently tear the paper away. For the inside logs, peel back the bottom left corner and drag your thumb under the paper along this edge to pop the stitches.

> **TIP:** Do not remove the paper from the center square at this time. During the quilt assembly process, you may change the setting several times. When your choice has been finalized, pencil in the row and block number on the paper squares. Log Cabin blocks can appear identical, so unless they are marked, it is impossible to tell the top from the bottom once they have been removed from the design wall. Numbering the squares keeps them oriented and will prevent sewing a row upside-down.

BLOCKS WITH ANGLED UNITS: Paper removal is more time-consuming with these blocks. A pair of fine tweezers is helpful for removing the smaller pieces of paper.

Warning: These blocks are very addictive – once you start making them, you won't want to stop. Especially the multi-fabric blocks! You will always want to make "just one more."

Discipline yourself to remove the paper after each block has been trimmed. It takes only a few minutes for one block, but it can take hours if you wait until all of them have been made. In addition, the blocks are easier to play with on the design wall when the paper has been removed.

Practice makes perfect!

Everyone has heard the expression, "Walk before you run." Begin with a "walk" through a traditional Log Cabin block. Once you have practiced and understood the construction and trimming of the basic block, then you can pick up the pace and move on to the blocks with angled units. All the blocks in this book are based on the Log Cabin. Perfect this block and you will easily master them all!

TIP: If the reversed seam is on the bottom when two blocks are sewn together, pin the seam allowance to prevent it from being stitched in the wrong direction. The seam will naturally revert to its original position if it isn't "persuaded" to go the other way.

Possibilities

The Log Cabin block lends itself to many design variations.

- For pictorial quilts, eliminate the light and dark side for full blocks of color within the design.
- SQUARE DANCE (page 120) does not look like a Log Cabin block, but it is. Choose a block with three or four rounds. Start with a dark center and alternate light and dark rounds (Fig. 2–25). For an easy but interesting design set, begin every other block with a light center.
- Select a 7" block and use a 4" (finished size) embroidered, appliquéd, or pieced block for the center square. You could also use this block to frame a quilt label.

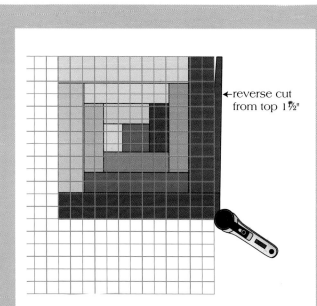

← reverse cut from top 1½"

Fig. 2–24. Start with a reverse cut at the top to ensure a square corner.

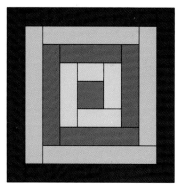

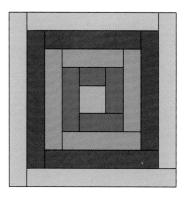

Fig. 2–25. Around the World Log Cabin blocks.

Chapter 3

Log Cabin Variations

There are many relatives in the Log Cabin family. The following block piecing instructions can be applied to blocks of any size.

Courthouse Steps

Courthouse Steps follows the same basic construction principles as the traditional Log Cabin block. However, the logs are added to opposite sides of the center square instead of being sewn in a clockwise rotation. The structure of the block is similar to a quarter-square triangle or Hourglass Block (Fig. 3–1).

The block is symmetrical, and its design structure is ideal for pictorial quilts. Select a block whose center square and logs are the same finished width for a smoother diagonal line.

When Courthouse Steps blocks are set together in a quilt, they can form a pattern that resembles Chinese lanterns (Fig. 3–2).

Any Log Cabin block can be easily converted to a Courthouse Steps block, as shown in Fig. 3–3.

Sewing the block

To speed up the piecing process, two logs can be placed and sewn consecutively. Depending on the size of the center square, it may be necessary to wait until one full round has been completed before sewing the rest of the logs consecutively. For blocks with a small center square, the bottom edge of B2 could accidentally be sewn in the seam allowance when B3 is attached.

- Secure A1 to the foundation with a fabric glue stick.
- Place, trim, and sew B2 and B3. Press the logs away from the center (Fig. 3–4). Pin down.
- Place, trim, and sew B4 and B5. Press the logs away from the center and pin down (Fig. 3–5).
- Position B6 and B7 (Fig. 3–6) and sew consecutively.
- Repeat this procedure for the remaining logs, changing to the wider strips for logs C10–C13. Backstitch at the beginning and end of logs C12 and C13.
- Courthouse Steps blocks are trimmed in the same manner as Log Cabin blocks. Refer to Trimming blocks on page 26 for detailed instructions.

COURTHOUSE STEPS

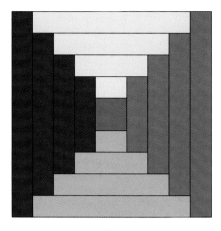

Fig. 3–1. Courthouse Steps block.

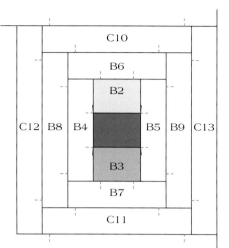

Fig. 3–4. Press logs away from the center square.

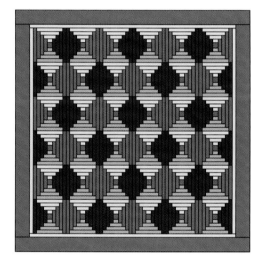

Fig. 3–2. The same Courthouse Steps block has been repeated over the entire quilt top. Can you find it?

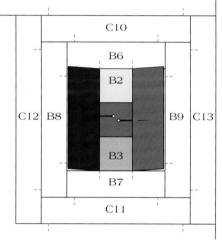

Fig. 3–5. Place fine straight pins in the seam folds to keep the logs flat.

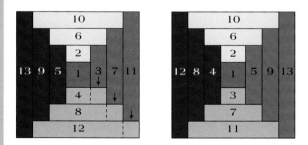

Fig. 3–3. Converting a Log Cabin block to a Courthouse Steps block: (a) extend the vertical lines on one side of the block; (b) erase the horizontal lines.

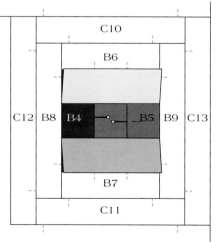

Fig. 3–6. Place logs B6 and B7 and sew them consecutively.

OFF-CENTER CONSTRUCTION

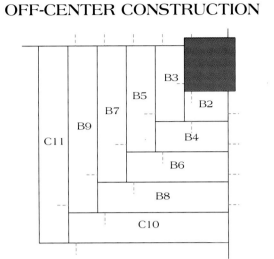

Fig. 3–7. The corner square extends ¼" past the outside pattern lines.

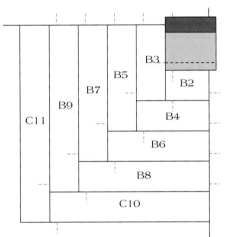

Fig. 3–8. Align B2 with the outside edge of the corner square.

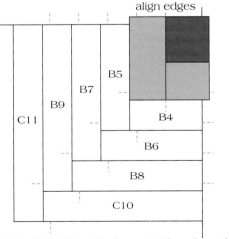

Fig. 3–9. Align B3 with the outside edge of the corner square.

Thick and Thin

 Thick and Thin is a Log Cabin variation that has wide logs on one side of the center square and narrow logs on the other. The finished block appears rounded. In a Thick and Thin block, the last log is thick. By itself, this block is rather ho-hum. It isn't until the blocks are rotated and placed side by side that the design possibilities begin to emerge. See SPINNING IN CIRCLES on page 120 for an example of a quilt made of Thick and Thin blocks.

Thin and Thick

In a Thin and Thick block, the last log is thin. This block was used in VICTORIAN TOPIARY on page 75 and BASKETS AND BLOOMS on page 83.

Off-Center

From basic Log Cabin block construction, you learned that the outside logs are cut wide and trimmed to size when the block is completed. In the Off-Center block, the corner square (A1) is considered an outside log; therefore, it extends ¼" past the pattern line on the two outside edges.

- Place a 1¾" square in position A1 on the foundation. Align the two inside fabric edges with the fabric placement lines and secure with a glue stick (Fig. 3–7).
- With right sides together, place B2 on top of A1 and trim B2 the same size as A1. Notice that B2 has one outside edge, so the fabric should extend ¼" past the pattern line. Start the stitching at the outside fabric edge, sew three stitches past the pattern line, backstitch to the line, then finish the seam (Fig. 3–8). Press B2 away from A1.
- Place B3 and trim the log ¼" past the pattern line, even with the outside fabric edge of A1 (Fig. 3–9). Start sewing at the inside fabric edge, sew to the pattern line, backstitch three stitches, then complete

the seam. Backstitch at the end of odd-numbered logs.

- Attach the remaining logs. Remember to change to a wide strip for logs C10 and C11.

Remember to backstitch at the beginning of even-numbered rows and at the end of odd-numbered rows.

Designing with Off-Center blocks

The Off-Center block is easy to make, goes together quickly, and has limitless possibilities.

- This block has the same design structure as a Log Cabin block, and when made half light and half dark, it can be used in any Log Cabin setting.
- Two Off-Center blocks and two mirror-image Off-Center blocks make perfect cornerstones for a "piano-key" border (see AUTUMN JEWELS on page 107).
- Eliminate the light side of the block and use the same fabric for each pair of adjacent logs. Turn the block on point for a chevron design.
- Reverse the light-to-dark fabric sequence on alternate blocks for a Lover's Knot block. You will need four Off-Center blocks to make one Lover's Knot block (Fig. 3–10).
- This block can also be made with a pieced or appliquéd block in the corner (Fig. 3–11).

Steps to the Cabin

 This block is a variation of the Off-Center block. The difference is that "step" squares are pieced to the odd-numbered logs before they are attached to the foundation (see COBBLESTONES, page 96). Refer to the sewing instructions for the Off-Center block for construction.

If all your Off-Center blocks are alike in fabric choices and placement, strip piecing is recommended. In cutting for strip piecing, be sure to include seam allowances. From the log fabric, cut

Fig. 3–10. Four Off-Center blocks set as a Lover's Knot.

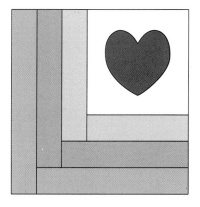

Fig. 3–11. Add appliqué or a small pieced block.

STEPS TO THE
CABIN CONSTRUCTION

Fig. 3–12. Sew a log strip and a step strip together, then cut segments from the joined strips.

Fig. 3–13. Press the seam allowances toward the log.

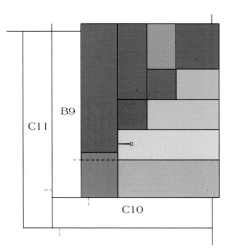

Fig. 3–14. Continue adding logs and log units. Remember to backstitch on the outside edges of the block.

a strip equal in width to the first log's length. From the step fabric, cut a strip the width of the steps. Join the log and step strips lengthwise. Press the seam allowances toward the log strip. Using the width of the log, cut the joined strips into segments (Fig. 3–12). Repeat for each log size.

Sewing the block

The following instructions apply to a single 6" block, but the method applies to a block of any size.

- Using a ¼" foot and 16–18 stitches per inch, sew a 1½" square to log B3 (1½" x 1¾"), B5 (1½" x 2¾"), B7 (1½" x 3¾"), and B9 (1½" x 4¾"), and a 1¾" square to C11 (1¾" x 5¾"). Press the seam allowances toward the logs, away from the squares (Fig. 3–13).
- Place a 1¾" square in the A1 position on the foundation. Align the two inside fabric edges with the fabric placement lines and secure with fabric glue. The two outside fabric edges will extend ¼" past the outside pattern lines.
- With right sides together, place B2 on top of A1 and trim B2 the same length as A1. B2 should extend ¼" past the outside pattern line. Use a walking foot to attach B2 to A1. Start at the outside edge, stitching toward the center of the block. This is an outside edge – remember to backstitch!
- Press the seam allowances away from A1.
- Place the B3 unit on top of A1 and B2, right sides together and matching seams. Secure the seam with a fine straight pin. Pin through the fabric layers only, not the paper. Start sewing at the inside edge, sewing toward the outside of the pattern. Backstitch at the end of the seam.
- Attach the remaining logs and units, backstitching at the start of even-numbered logs and the end of odd-numbered logs (Fig. 3–14).
- Follow the block trimming sequence on the pattern.

Single Tulip

Use a scant seam allowance to attach C4, C5, F10 and F11 (pattern on page 38). Use a full seam allowance to attach the D and G background triangles. The full seam allowance guarantees you will not lose the point in the seam allowances when blocks are joined. For a scant seam allowance, sew one needle-width to the right of the stitching guideline, and for a full seam allowance, sew one needle-width to the left of the stitching guideline.

Sewing the block

- Sew A1, B2, B3, C4, and C5 as you would a traditional Log Cabin block (Fig. 3–15).

- Scissor-cut logs C4 and C5 just inside the angled line. Eye-ball the cut, fold the fabric along the guideline to create a cutting line, or draw the cutting line in pencil. The angled line should be visible to ensure accurate fabric placement for the next log. Place a fine straight pin in the seam allowances of C5 to keep it flat (Fig. 3–16).

- The D and G half-square triangles are similar in size (sizes given in pattern). Select the two smaller triangles and place one right side down on the angled fabric placement line of D6. Place the other one on D7.

- Insert the needle one needle-width to the left of the stitching guideline and sew D6. At the end of the seam, lift the needle and presser foot and, without cutting the threads, rotate the block and sew D7 (Fig. 3–17). Cut the top and bottom connecting threads.

- Press the triangles away from logs C4 and C5. Place a fine straight pin in the seam allowance fold to keep the triangles flat. These small triangles have a tendency to pop up if not secured.

- Do a point check before adding logs E8 and E9. Change to a wide strip and attach E8 and E9, backstitching at the start of E9.

SINGLE TULIP CONSTRUCTION

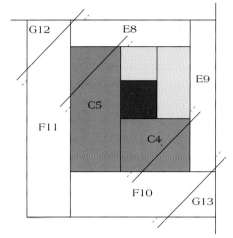

Fig. 3–15. Sew the center square and the first round of logs as usual.

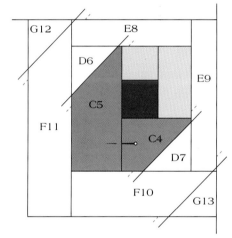

Fig. 3–16. Cut just inside the angled line and pin down C5.

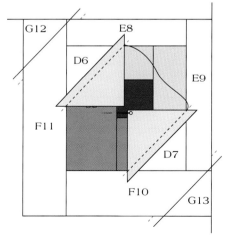

Fig. 3–17. Sew the first triangle, then rotate the block without cutting any threads, to sew the second triangle.

MULTIPLE
SINGLE TULIP BLOCKS

If you are making multiple blocks, it is more convenient to rotary cut than scissor cut the angles on C4, C5, F10, and F11. First, cut the following lengths from the C and F strips:

C4 – 2⅝"
C5 – scant 4⅛"
F10 – 5"
F11 – 6¾"

With right sides together, place C4 on top of C5 with the right side edges aligned as shown in the figure. Position the 45-degree ruler line on the bottom edge of the strips. Align the ¼" line with the lower-right corner for the seam allowances. Cut the angle. Repeat for F10 and F11.

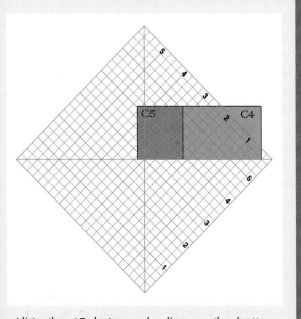

Align the 45-degree ruler line on the bottom edge and the ¼" line on the lower-right corner.

- Place, trim, and sew F10 and F11. F11 should extend ¼" past the outside pattern line at the straight end. This is an outside edge; remember to backstitch. Trim F10 and F11 on the angled fabric placement lines. Place a fine straight pin in the seam allowance of F11 to keep it flat.
- Repeat the inside triangle procedure to add the outside G triangles. These are outside pieces, and it is necessary to backstitch at the pattern lines. Press the triangles away from the block center.

> **TIP:** When sewing outside diagonal logs, reduce the stitch length to 18–20 stitches per inch. This eliminates the need to backstitch. Of course, these small stitches are very difficult to remove. I recommend perfecting the placement of the outside triangle before using this tip.

Trimming the block

The trimming for this block and any block with points is a little different from a block with straight logs. Before making the first and second cuts, it is necessary to make sure there is ¼" between the point and the ruler edge.

FIRST CUT – Place a square ruler on top of the foundation block. Align the ruler's edge on the extension lines. Check where the tip of the point is in relation to the ¼" mark on the ruler. If the tip is outside the seam allowance, make the cut. If the tip is inside the seam allowance, adjust the position of the ruler until the tip of the point lies just to the left of the ¼" mark. Make the cut. Having the point a generous ¼" from the fabric edge guarantees a sharp, flat point when two blocks are sewn together with an exact ¼" seam allowance (Fig. 3–18).

SECOND CUT – Rotate the block a quarter-turn clockwise. Place a horizontal ruler line on the just-cut fabric edge and adjust the vertical ruler edge until the point rests just to the left of the ¼" mark (Fig. 3–19). Cut.

THIRD CUT – Rotate the block a quarter-turn clockwise. Measure from the left edge of the block to make the third cut. For example, with a 6½" block (includes seam allowances), you would place the 6½" ruler line on the left edge of the block. Cut.

FOURTH CUT – Rotate the block a quarter-turn clockwise. Align the top ruler edge on the top block edge. Use the block's measurements to align the ruler with the bottom and left edges. For example, align the ruler's horizontal and vertical 6½" ruler lines with the bottom and left edges of the block. Make the final cut. Remove the paper and trim the ears.

Adding folded corner squares

A simple and effective design element that will dramatically change Log Cabin, Courthouse Steps, and Off-Center blocks is the addition of triangles to the logs.

The folded squares are placed in the corner at the completion of a full round. The triangles are secured with a fabric glue stick and attached to the block when the next log is added. The triangles are secured on the sides only. The diagonal folded line is loose. When attached, the folded square resembles a small triangular pocket.

The triangles can be any size you choose. They can cover one seam, one-and-a-half seams, or two seams. The size of the triangles can vary within each block, getting progressively bigger from the center to the outside edge. Place the triangles in a single diagonal line or form an "X" with two diagonal lines.

It is easy to determine the size of square to cut for the triangles.

continues on page 40

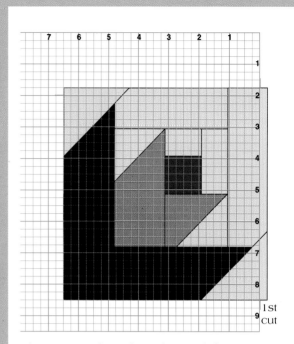

Fig. 3–18. Adjust the ruler until the point rests just to the left of the ¼" mark.

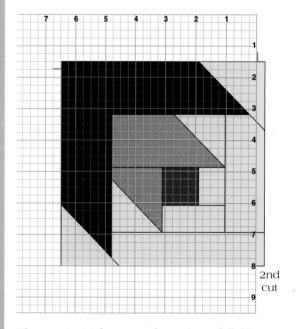

Fig. 3–19. Make sure there is a full ¼" seam allowance beyond the point.

6" Single Tulip Block

6" Single Tulip
  Trim block to 6½".

Strip widths
  A – 1¾" square
  B – 1⅜" strip
  C – 2" strip

D – 2⅜" square
E – 1⅝" strip
F – 2¼" strip
G – 2⅞" square
For special cutting instructions, see page 37.

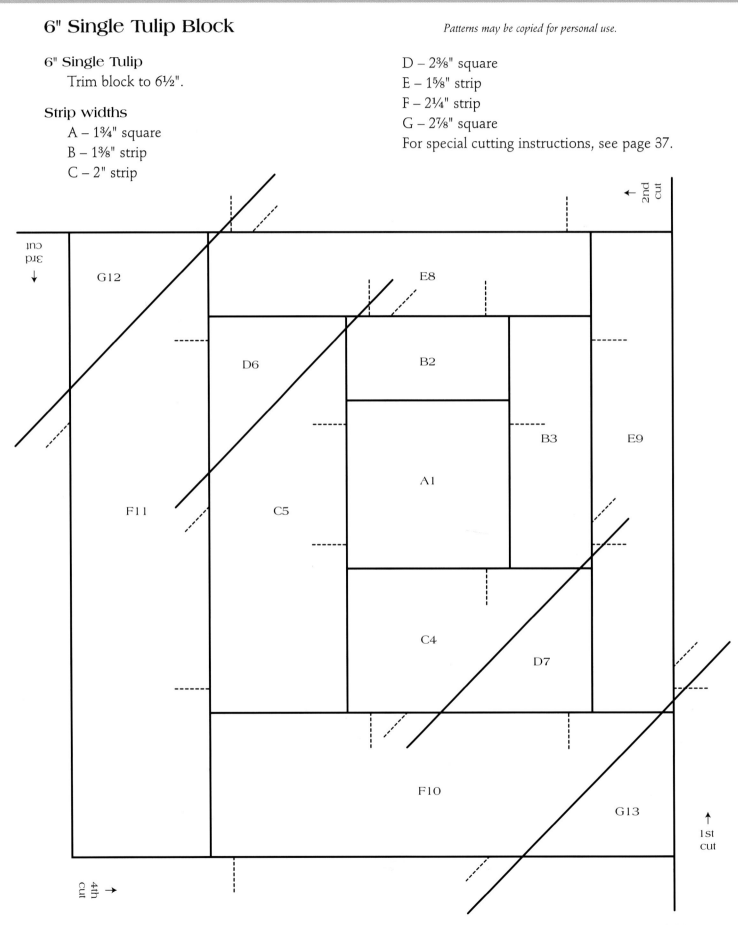

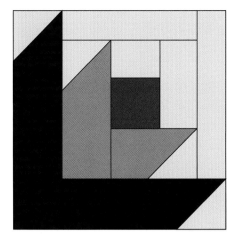

6" SINGLE TULIP fabric placement guide.

TULIP BOUQUET table runner (20½" x 54"), pieced and machine quilted by the author. This quilt is made from 12 – 6" Log Cabin blocks and 4 – 6" Single Tulip blocks (see Teaching Guide, Lesson 2, page 127).

ADDING FOLDED TRIANGLES

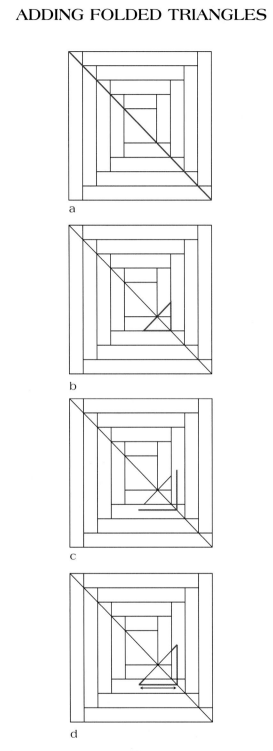

a

b

c

d

Fig. 3–20. (a) Draw a line corner to corner. (b) Draw the triangle placement. (c) Add ¼" to both short sides. (d) Connect the diagonal line to the ¼" extensions. Measure the short side of the larger triangle to find the size square to cut.

- On the foundation, draw a corner-to-corner diagonal line in one direction or both directions, depending on the placement of the triangles (Fig. 3–20a).
- Using a clear acrylic ruler, align any vertical ruler line with the drawn diagonal line and mark the exact position and size of the triangle on the foundation block (Fig. 3–20b).
- Use the ¼" line of the ruler to add ¼" to both short sides of the triangle (Fig. 3–20c).
- Extend the long side of the triangle to connect with the two ¼" extension lines. The measurement of a short side is the exact size to cut the square (Fig. 3–20d). The block is trimmed to size before the outside triangles are added so it is not necessary to increase the size of these triangles.

This technique is best suited to wallhangings, which will not receive much use. Triangles made from larger squares may sag over time if they are added to quilts that will be used every day.

Courthouse Steps with Triangles

 Use the following step-by-step instructions for adding folded triangles to a 6" Courthouse Steps block with four rounds of logs. (Use the instructions on page 31 to convert the Log Cabin pattern on page 85 to Courthouse Steps.) Select a light fabric for the logs and a dark fabric for the center square and folded squares. Cut eight 1¾" squares for the folded triangles.

Sewing the block

- With wrong sides together, press the 1¾" squares diagonally in half.
- Use fabric glue to secure the center square, then add logs B2, B3, B4, and B5. Pin down B4 and B5.
- Place a small amount of fabric glue in the top corner of B4 and position the first triangle. Align the triangle's sides with the pattern lines (Fig. 3–21).
- Add B6. The triangle is now secured on one side.

- Repeat this procedure to add a triangle in the bottom corner of B5.
- Add B8 and B9. The triangles are secured on both sides when B8 and B9 are added (Fig. 3–22).
- Add the remaining logs. Remember to change to a wide strip for the outermost logs.

Trimming the block

The block is trimmed to size before the corner triangles are added, and the paper is still in place when the final triangles are attached.

- Trim the block to size. Then use a fabric glue stick to secure a triangle in the top corner of C16, placing the diagonal fold on the corner of the preceding triangle. When the triangle is accurately positioned, unfold the triangle and sew a diagonal seam ½" from the fold line as shown (Fig. 3–23).
- Repeat this procedure to position a triangle in the bottom corner of C17.

Leaving the top layer of the triangle free makes it possible to adjust the side length for a perfect match when connecting two blocks.

To reduce seam bulk when the blocks are sewn together, you may want to trim the middle layer. Do not trim the bottom layer because it will keep the corners square.

Simple Pineapple Block

This Pineapple block is simple to construct (see pattern on page 113) because all the rounds are made from straight logs. There are no half-square triangles in the inside logs.

The strips for this block are similar in size. Be careful not to mix them up!

Sewing the block

- Secure the center square with a fabric glue stick applied to the foundation.

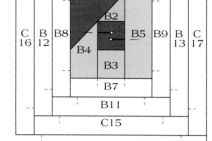

Fig. 3–21. The diagonal seam rests on the corner of the center square. Pin down logs B4 and B5.

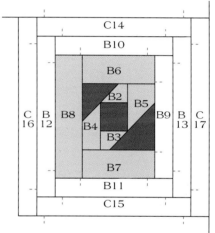

Fig. 3–22. The top triangle is secured by logs B6 and B8. The addition of B9 will finish securing the lower triangle.

Fig. 3–23. Unfold the triangle and sew a diagonal seam ½" from the fold line (toward the corner of the block).

PINEAPPLE CONSTRUCTION

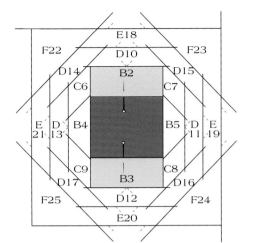

Fig. 3–24. Press B2 and B3 away from the center square. Pin down the logs.

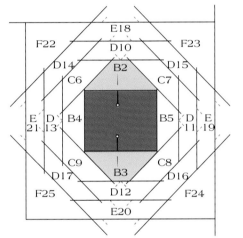

Fig. 3–25. Trim B2 and B3 inside the angled lines.

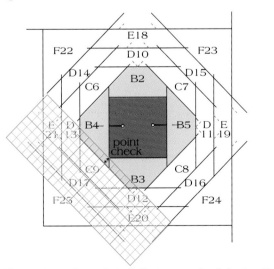

Fig. 3–26. Completed first round of logs. Be sure to point check before adding next round.

- Position and trim logs B2 and B3 the same length as the center square.
- Insert the needle into the stitching guideline and attach B2, lift the needle and the presser foot and, without cutting the threads, rotate the block and attach B3.
- Clip the connecting threads top and bottom, and press logs B2 and B3 away from the center square (Fig. 3–24).
- Trim both ends of logs B2 and B3 inside the angled fabric placement lines. Place a fine straight pin in the seam allowance fold to keep the logs flat (Fig. 3–25).
- Repeat this procedure for B4 and B5, removing the straight pins in B2 and B3 before pressing B4 and B5. Pin down B4 and B5 (Fig. 3–26).

Now the piecing process really speeds up. Four logs can be trimmed and sewn consecutively. I refer to this as "loading up" the block.

Point check before adding C6, C7, C8, and C9. Adjust the stitching guideline if necessary. This is the only time you will have to point check this block.

- Place and trim C6, C7, C8, and C9. Use the full length of the fabric placement line as a cutting guide. Insert the needle into the stitching guideline and sew C6, lift the needle and presser foot, rotate the block and sew C7. Repeat for C8 and C9.
- Press C6, C7, C8, and C9 away from the center and trim the ends even with the vertical and horizontal fabric placement lines. Pin down all four logs (Fig. 3–27).
- Place D10, D11, D12, and D13 (Fig. 3–28). Sew the logs consecutively.
- Repeat this procedure for the remaining logs. Remember to change to a wide strip for logs E18, E19, E20, and E21. Center the four outside triangles on the extended fabric placement lines. These are outside pieces, and it is necessary to either sew with a shorter stitch or backstitch at the pattern lines.

Trimming the block

The cutting sequence is the same as the Log Cabin block.

Wild Goose Chase

The construction of this block is similar to Courthouse Steps because the logs are added to opposite sides of the center square (see pattern on page 114).

Sewing the block

- To make the B, C, and F triangles, cut squares the size given in the pattern. Cut the squares in half diagonally.
- Secure the center square with a small dab of a fabric glue stick.
- Place triangles B2 and B3 on the center square.
- Sew B2, then lift the needle and the presser foot and, without cutting the connecting threads, rotate the block and attach B3.
- Cut the connecting threads top and bottom and press B2 and B3 away from the center. Pin down the logs with a fine straight pin.
- Add triangles B4 and B5 in the same manner and press. Pin down the triangles and trim the ears with a rotary cutter.
- Place the ¼" line of a clear acrylic ruler on the next fabric placement line and do a point check.
- Add the C6–C9 triangles as you did the B triangles. Press the triangles back and trim the ears. The block now resembles a double square-in-a-square (Fig. 3–29).
- Pre-cut logs D10 and D11 the same length as the double square-in-a-square. Place and sew the logs. Press them away from the center and trim them just inside the diagonal lines.
- Pre-cut logs D12 and D13 the same length as the fabric placement lines. Sew, press, and trim on the diagonal lines (Fig. 3–30, page 44).

WILD GOOSE CHASE CONSTRUCTION

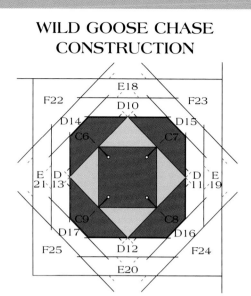

Fig. 3–27. Press logs away from the center and pin them down.

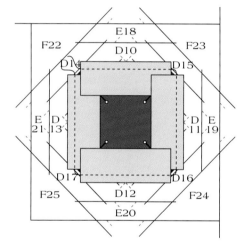

Fig. 3–28. Add logs D10, D11, D12, and D13 by sewing consecutively.

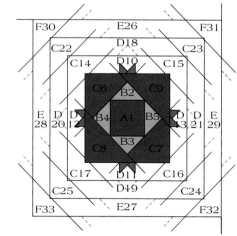

Fig. 3–29. Two rounds completed.

WILD GOOSE CHASE
CONSTRUCTION
continued

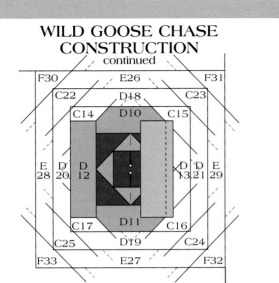

Fig. 3–30. Log D12 is ready to trim. Log D13 is ready to press and trim.

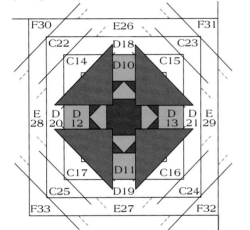

Fig. 3–31. Triangles C14–C17 are ready to sew.

SQUARE-IN-A-SQUARE

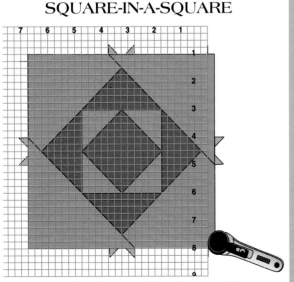

Fig. 3–32. Check to see that there are ¼" seam allowances for the left and right points.

- Do a point check, then position triangles C14–C17 (Figure 3–31). Sew consecutively. The ears can be trimmed now or later when the paper is removed.
- Repeat this procedure for the remaining logs. Remember to change to a wide strip for E26–E29.
- Sew the F30–F33 triangles to the corners.

Trimming the block

The trimming procedure is identical to a Log Cabin block.

Square-in-a-Square Block

 Square-in-a-Square has full rounds of light and dark values (see pattern on page 112). The diagonal pieces are added as half-square triangles instead of logs.

Sewing the block

- Position light triangles B2 and B3 on the fabric placement lines. Sew B2, lift the needle and presser foot, rotate the block, and sew B3. Trim the connecting threads. Press the triangles away from the center and pin them down at the fold.
- Repeat for light triangles B4 and B5. Trim the ears with a rotary cutter. Place the ¼" mark of a clear acrylic ruler on the next fabric placement line and do a point check. Follow the numbered rotation to complete the block.

Trimming the block

FIRST CUT: Place a square ruler on the block and align the right edge with the cutting extension lines. Keeping the ruler straight, adjust the ruler position until the ¼" line is aligned with the point on the right side of the block. Using the block measurements, including seam allowances, check where the left point is. For example, in a 6½" block, check where the left point is in relation to the 6¼" mark on the ruler. Adjust the ruler until both points will finish equally distant from the fabric edge, but not less than ¼" (Fig. 3–32). Make the cut.

SECOND CUT: Rotate the block a quarter-turn clockwise and repeat the cutting procedure used for the first cut.

THIRD CUT: Rotate the block a quarter-turn clockwise. Using the block size, measure from the left edge of the block to make the cut.

FOURTH CUT: Repeat the instructions for making the third cut.

TIP: If it is obvious that you will lose one or both points when the block is trimmed, go back and increase the seam allowances by a needle's width on the last two triangles. Increasing the seam allowances will bring the points in from the fabric edge, closer to the center of the block. Then the points will not be lost when the block is trimmed to size.

MATCHING POINTS

Insert a pin through both points to be matched. To avoid shifting the points during pinning, pinch the triangles together, leaving the "matching pin" perpendicular to the fabrics. Place a securing pin on each side of the matching pin, then secure the matching pin. Remove each pin just before it reaches the presser foot. For increased accuracy and control, reduce the sewing machine speed.

Sew with a ¼" seam allowance and stitch through the "X" created by the sewing lines. For the sharpest points, run the stitching line through the top of the "X" just a thread or two above the "X." Inspect the points, and if they appear to be "floating" away from the seam line, re-sew the seam with a wider seam allowance.

Insert a pin through both points.

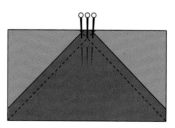

With the matching pins perpendicular to the fabric pieces, secure the point with two more pins.

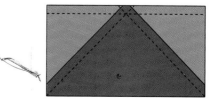

Sew through the "X" created by the seam lines.

Chapter 4

Feature Quilt Patterns

COUNTRY CHARM, pieced by the author and machine quilted by
Carol Seeley of Campbell River, B.C., Canada.

Finished quilt size 60½" x 72½"
Quilt size before borders 48" x 60"
Eighty 6" Log Cabin blocks, three rounds

Fabric Requirements
Based on 42"-wide fabric.

Fabric	Yards
Center squares	¼
Light 1	½
Light 2	¾
Light 3	1⅜
Dark 1	⅝
Dark 2	⅞
Dark 3	1⅜
Inner border	½
Outer border:	
cut crosswise	1⅛
OR lengthwise	2*
Binding	⅝
Backing:	
crosswise seam	4
OR lengthwise	4½

*2½ yards for a directional print

Cutting Instructions
- Cut strips from selvage to selvage.
- Center Squares: Cut four 1⅝" A strips and crosscut them into 80 1⅝" squares.
- Light 1 & 2 and Dark 1 & 2: Cut B strips a generous 1¼" as needed.
- Light 3 and Dark 3: Cut C strips a 1⅝" as needed.

PRE-CUT LOGS: Strip widths are given with the pattern. The logs can be cut to size as you sew or pre-cut to individual lengths as follows:

LIGHT FABRICS:

B2	1⅝"
B3	2⅜"
B6	3¼"
B7	4"
C10	4⅞"
C11	5⅞"

DARK FABRICS:

B4	2⅜"
B5	3¼"
B8	4"
B9	4⅞"
C12	5⅞"
C13	7"

Quilt Assembly
- Make 80 copies of the 6" Log Cabin block with three rounds on page 50.
- Foundation piece the blocks (see Foundation Piecing, page 15).
- Secure the seam allowances with a small dab of fabric glue applied with a toothpick to prevent them from shifting as you sew.

Barn Raising setting
- Refer to the Quilt Assembly diagram and quilt photo for block placement. Use a ¼" foot and stitch length set at 12 stitches to the inch or 2.0 to join blocks in 10 rows of eight each.
- Press seam allowances in one direction in even-numbered rows and in the opposite direction in odd-numbered rows.
- Sew the rows together. Press seam allowances downward between rows.

Inner border

- Cut six 1¾" strips from the fabric width. Remove the selvages from all the strips.
- Cut two strips in half. Sew a half strip to each full strip. Press seam allowances open.
- Measure the length of the quilt through the center and trim two pieced strips to this size. Pin the borders in place and sew. Press seam allowances toward the border.
- Measure the width of the quilt through the center, including the side borders, and trim two pieced strips this size. Pin and sew. Press seam allowances toward the border.

Outer border

- For borders cut on the length of grain, cut four 5½" strips.
- For borders cut on the cross grain, cut six 5½" strips. Attach the outer border strips as you did the inner border.

> **TIP:** For a directional border fabric cut on the length of the grain, cut three 5½" strips from the cross grain for the top and bottom borders before cutting the side borders from the fabric length.

Finishing

- Layer the backing, batting, and quilt top; baste. Quilt the layers (see Quilting Options on page 118 for ideas).
- Use seven 2¼" strips to bind the raw edges.

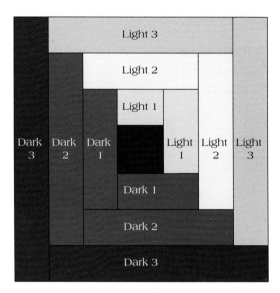

Fabric placement guide

Quilt assembly

COUNTRY CHARM

Patterns may be copied for personal use.

6" Log Cabin with Three Rounds
   Trim block to 6½".

To cut a generous 1¼" strip, position the fabric edge halfway between the ¼" and ⅜" ruler mark.

STRIP WIDTHS
   A – scant 1⅝" square
   B – generous 1¼" strip
   C – 1⅝" strip

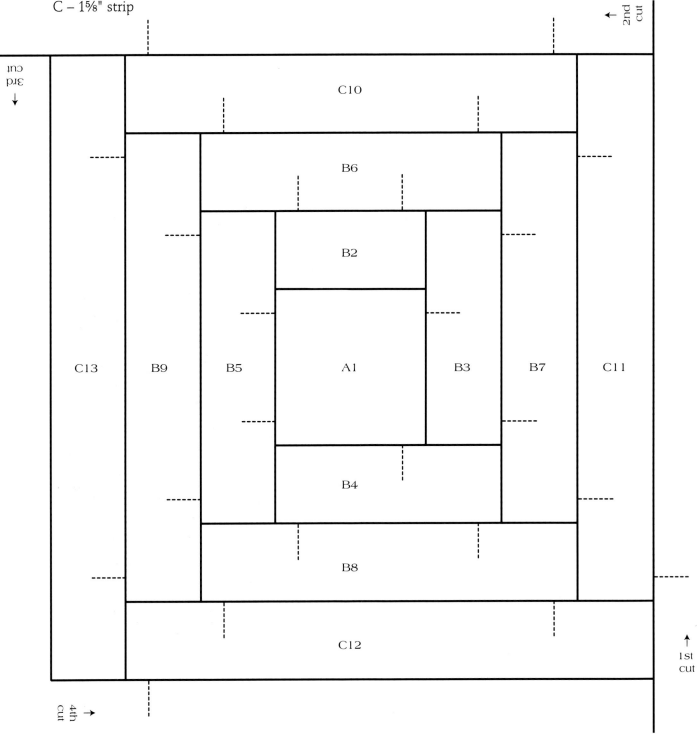

Sweet Dreams Baby Quilt

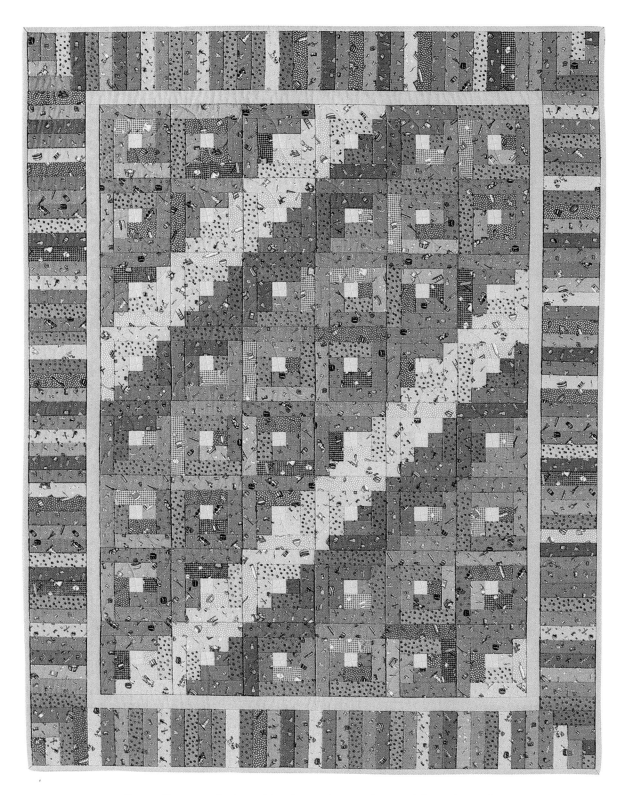

SWEET DREAMS, designed by the author and Jean Fisher of Langley,
B.C., Canada; pieced and machine quilted by the author.

Finished quilt size 40" x 50"
Quilt size before borders 30" x 40"
Forty-eight 5" Log Cabin blocks,
    two rounds
Two 4" Off-Center blocks
Two 4" mirror-image Off-Center blocks

Fabric Requirements
Based on 42"-wide fabric.

Blocks and piano-key border: For each of the following color groups, buy ¼ yard of each fabric. Leftovers will be used for the piano-key border:

five assorted blues
five assorted yellows
five assorted pinks
five assorted greens
five assorted violets

Fabric	Yards
Center squares	¼
Inner border	¼
Binding	⅜
Backing	1⅝

Cutting Instructions
- Cut strips selvage to selvage.
- Log Cabin A squares: Cut two 1½" strips and crosscut them into 48 – 1½" squares.
- Cut four 1¾" off-center A squares from any of the 1¾" strips.

Logs: Cut one 1½" B strip and one 1¾" C strip from each fabric. Cut more strips as needed.

Quilt Assembly
- Make 48 copies of the 5" Log Cabin block with Two Rounds on page 54.
- Foundation piece the 48 blocks, making the color combinations as shown in Fig. 4–1 (refer to Foundation Piecing on page 15).
- Make two 4" Off-Center blocks (page 55) and two 4" mirror-image Off-Center blocks for the border corners (see mirror-image instructions under Transfer pen, page 15).

Straight Furrows setting
- Refer to the Quilt Assembly diagram and quilt photo for block placement. Use a ¼" foot and stitch length set at 12 stitches to the inch or 2.0 to join blocks in eight rows of six each.
- Press seam allowances in one direction in even-numbered rows and in the opposite direction in odd-numbered rows.
- Sew the rows together. Press the seam allowances downward between rows.

Inner border
- Cut four 1½" strips from the width of the fabric.
- Measure the length of the quilt through the center and trim two strips this size. Pin the borders in place and sew. Press seam allowances away from the quilt top.
- Measure the width of the quilt top through the center, including side borders, and trim the two remaining strips this size. Pin and sew. Press seam allowances away from the quilt top.

Piano-key border

- Refer to Piano-Key Border on page 117 for detailed instructions. Cut strips 1½" wide. Cut the sewn piano-key borders 4½" wide.
- Add the side borders to the quilt and press the seam allowances toward the inner border.
- Refer to the quilt photo for accurate positioning of the blocks. Sew the Off-Center blocks to the ends of the top and bottom borders and add these borders to the quilt. Press seam allowances toward the inner border.

Finishing

- Layer the backing, batting, and quilt top; baste. Quilt the layers (see Quilting Options on page 118 for ideas).
- Use five 2¼" strips to bind the raw edges.

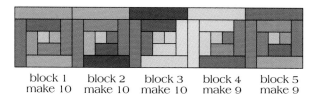

block 1	block 2	block 3	block 4	block 5
make 10	make 10	make 10	make 9	make 9

Fig. 4–1. Make the blocks in each color combination.

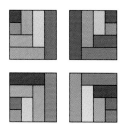

Fabric placement guide for corners

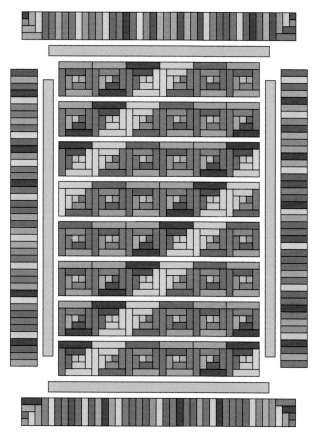

Quilt assembly

Sweet Dreams Baby Quilt

5" Log Cabin with Two Rounds

Trim block to 5½".

Strip widths

A – 1½" square

B – 1½" strip

C – 1¾" strip

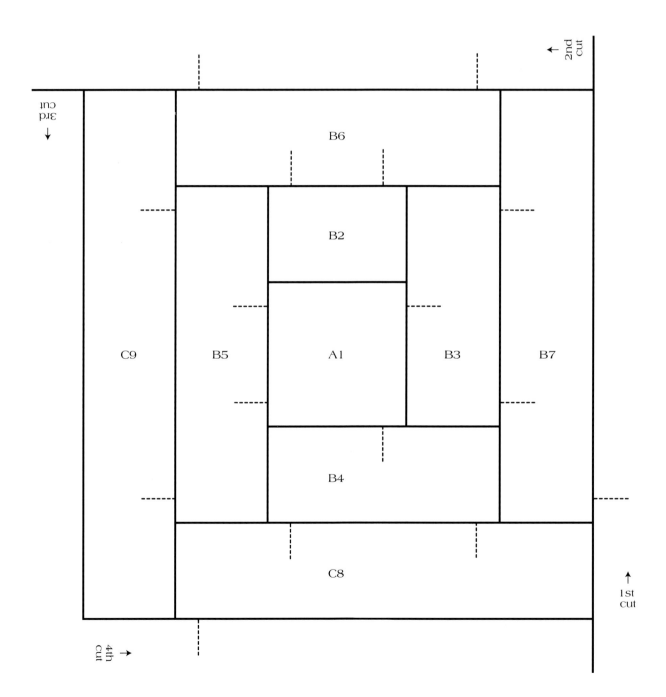

4" Off-Center Block

Trim block to 4½".

Strip widths

A – 1¾" square
B – 1½" strip
C – 1¾" strip

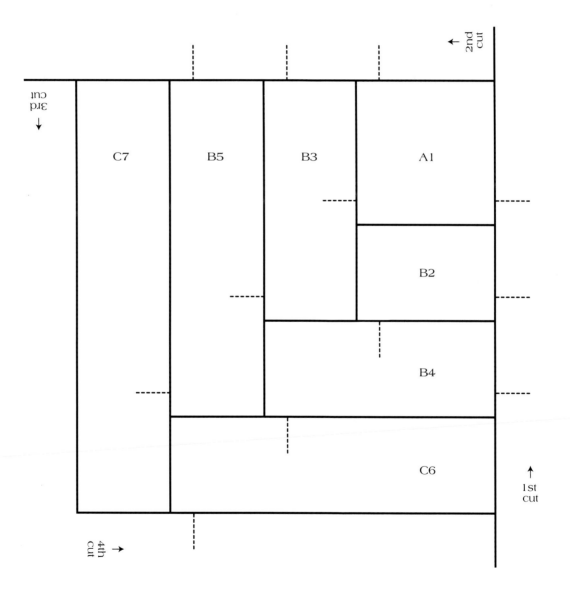

MOUNTAIN RETREAT

MOUNTAIN RETREAT, designed by the author; pieced by Sabina Granbois of Surrey, B.C., Canada; and machine quilted by Carol Seeley of Campbell River, B.C., Canada.

Finished quilt size 54" x 54"
Quilt size before borders 42½" x 42½"
Twenty-four 6" Log Cabin, four rounds

Fabric Requirements
Based on 42"-wide fabric.

LIGHTS: assorted fabrics, for logs and half-square triangles, to total 1⅓ yards
DARKS: assorted fabrics for logs to total 1 yard

Fabric	Yards
Center squares	⅛
Dark half-square triangles for blocks	½
Light background setting triangles and border 3	1½
Border 2 dark	½
Border 3 medium (small triangles)	⅓
Border 3 dark (large triangles)	⅝
Binding	½
Backing	3½

Cutting Instructions
- From the background fabric, cut four 2¼" strips on the length of grain for Border 1 before cutting the large squares for the side and corner triangles.
- Cut the rest of the strips selvage to selvage.

- For the center squares (A1), cut one 1½" strip and cross-cut it into 24 – 1½" squares.
- Cut one 1⅛" B strip and one 1⅜" C strip from all the light fabrics for logs.
- Cut one 1⅛" B strip and one 1⅜" C strip from all the dark fabrics for logs.
- Sawtooth border for blocks: Cut 96 – 2⅜" squares from a variety of light fabrics and 96 2⅜" squares from the dark fabric for making the half-square triangles. Cut 24 – 2" squares from a variety of light fabrics for the corners.

Quilt Assembly
- Make 24 copies of the 6" Log Cabin block with four rounds on page 61.
- Foundation piece the 24 blocks (see Foundation Piecing, page 15).
- Make 192 half-squares from the light and dark 2⅜" squares.
- Notice that the half-squares are sewn to the dark logs. Refer to the Block Assembly diagram for correct placement and join four half-squares. Press seam allowances toward the dark triangle.
- Pin and sew the four half-squares to the block. Press seam allowances away from the Log Cabin block.
- For the other side of the block, join a 2" light square and four half-squares. Press seam allowances toward the dark triangle.

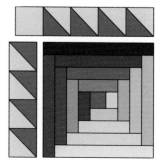

Block assembly

MAKING HALF-SQUARES

In pencil, draw a diagonal line on the wrong side of the light-colored 2⅜" squares.

With right sides together, place a light square on top of a dark square.

Align the edge of a ¼" foot with the drawn pencil line and sew the squares together.

At the fabric edge, rotate the squares and repeat for the other side of the line.

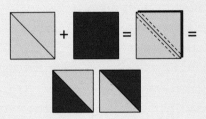

Draw a diagonal line and sew ¼" on both sides of the lines.

Place a ruler on the drawn line and rotary cut on the line.

Press seam allowances toward the dark fabric.

The measurement of the unfinished square is 2".

- Pin and sew this unit to the block. Press seam allowances away from the Log Cabin block.
- Repeat this procedure to make borders for all the Log Cabin blocks.
- Cut two 11⅞" background squares and cut them twice on the diagonal to yield eight side triangles.
- Cut two 11½" background squares and cut them once on the diagonal to yield four corner triangles.
- Use the Quilt Assembly diagram as a guide and position the blocks, side triangles, and corner triangles on a design wall or other flat surface.
- Sew the blocks and side triangles together in diagonal rows. Press seam allowances in one direction for even-numbered rows and in the opposite direction for odd-numbered rows.
- Sew the rows together. Press the seam allowances downward between rows.
- Add the corner triangles. The quilt now measures 43" x 43". Press seam allowances toward the corner triangles.

Borders 1 and 2

- From the dark Border-2 fabric, cut five 1½" strips across the grain. Remove the selvages from all the strips, cut one strip in quarters, and add one of the quarters to each of the long strips. Press seam allowances open.
- Join the 2¼" background strips and the 1½" dark strips on one long edge. Repeat for the remaining pairs of strips. Press seam allowances toward the dark border. Center the border strips on the quilt top. Take care that the background fabric is on the inside when the border units are attached. Miter the corners.

Border 3

- The shaded sawtooth square is made up of one half-square triangle and two quarter-square triangles. Use the quick-piecing method to make 32 shaded sawtooth squares and 32 mirror-image squares (Fig. 4–2).

Fig. 4–2. Sawtooth square and mirror image.

> **TIP:** An unfinished sawtooth square is 3½". It's a good idea to make a sample square to test this measurement. If the square measures less than 3½", decrease the seam allowance width or increase the square size. Many quilters prefer to make a larger square and then trim it to size.

- For the quilt's corners, use the half-square method to make four half-squares from the 3⅞" squares cut from fabrics 1 and 2.
- Lay the quilt top on a large flat surface or your design wall and position 16 shaded sawtooth squares on each of the four sides. Refer to the quilt assembly diagram and quilt photo for accurate placement. Place a half-square triangle block in each of the corners.
- Sew 16 shaded sawtooth squares together for each border. Sew borders to the sides of the quilt. Press seam allowances toward the inner border.
- Sew half-squares to each end of the remaining shaded sawtooth borders. Sew the borders to the top and bottom of the quilt. Press the seam allowances toward the inner border.

Finishing

- Layer the backing, batting, and quilt top; baste. Quilt the layers (see Quilting Options on page 118 for ideas).
- Use six 2¼" strips to bind the raw edges.

QUICK PIECING SHADED SAWTOOTH SQUARES

Cutting

LIGHT BACKGROUND (FABRIC 1): Cut 16 4¼" squares and two 3⅞" squares.

MEDIUM (FABRIC 2): Cut 16 – 4¼" squares and two 3⅞" squares

DARK (FABRIC 3): Cut 32 – 3⅞" squares.

Sawtooth Assembly

- Make 32 half-squares from the 4¼" fabric-1 and and fabric-2 squares (see Making Half-Squares, page 58).
- Place a half-square on top of a 3⅞" fabric-3 square, right sides together. Following the half-square method, draw a line from corner to corner in the opposite direction from the existing seam. Sew ¼" on either side of the diagonal line. Cut the squares on the line to yield 64 shaded sawtooth squares.

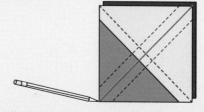

Sew diagonal seams opposite the existing seam.

Quilt assembly

6" Log Cabin with 4 rounds

Trim block to 6½".

Strip widths

A – 1½" square
B – 1⅛" strip
C – 1⅜" strip

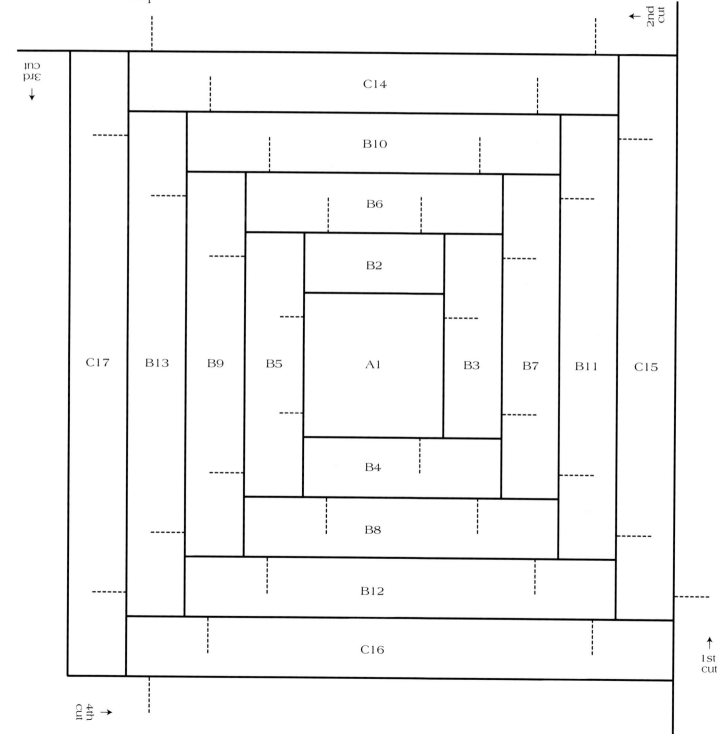

PINEAPPLE RHAPSODY

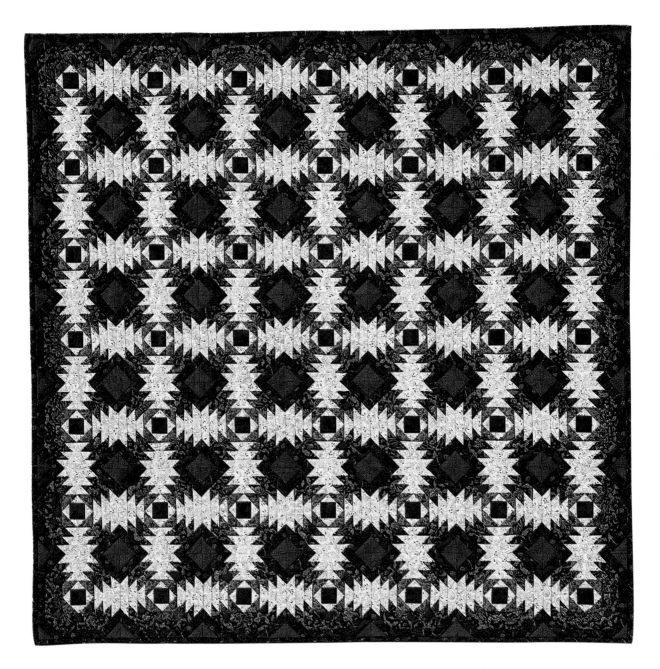

PINEAPPLE RHAPSODY, pieced by the author and machine quilted by
Carol Seeley of Campbell River, B.C., Canada.

Finished quilt size 42" x 42"
Forty-nine 6" Pineapple blocks,
  four rounds

Fabric Requirements
Based on 42"-wide fabric.

Fabric	Yards
Center squares	¼
Light	1⅝
Dark 1	½
Dark 2	⅝
Dark 3	¾
Dark 4	1
Corners	⅝
Binding	½
Backing	2¾

Cutting Instructions
- Cut strips selvage to selvage.
- Cut three scant 1¾" A strips and crosscut them into 49 scant 1¾" squares. Cut five generous 1⅝" B strips from the light fabric and crosscut them into 98 generous 1⅝" squares.
- Cut seven 2⅝" E strips from the corner fabric and crosscut them into 98 – 2⅝" squares.
- Cut the B and E squares in half on the diagonal to make half-square triangles.
- Cut the light and dark C strips and light D strips as needed. The strip widths are given with the pattern on page 65.

If you are making a planned Pineapple quilt in which all the blocks are alike, you can pre-cut the logs to the following lengths:

Light fabrics

D10–D13	2¼"
D18–D21	2¾"
E26–E29	3¼"

Dark fabrics

Dark 1	2¼"
Dark 2	2¾"
Dark 3	3¼"
Dark 4	4¼"

After sewing the logs to the foundation, trim them just inside the diagonal lines. Remember to point check before adding the third and fourth rounds.

Quilt Assembly
Follow the instructions for making a Wild Goose Chase block on page 43 to make the first round. Then refer to the Pineapple instructions on page 41 to complete the block.

- Make 49 copies of the 6" Pineapple block with four rounds on page 65.
- Referring to Fig. 4–3, make 25 center blocks (a), 20 side blocks (b), and four corner blocks (c).
- Refer to the Quilt Assembly diagram and quilt photo for block placement. Use a ¼" foot and stitch length set at 12 stitches to the inch or 2.0 to join blocks in seven rows of seven each.
- Press seam allowances in one direction in even-numbered rows and in the opposite direction in odd-numbered rows.
- Sew the rows together. Press seam allowances downward between rows.

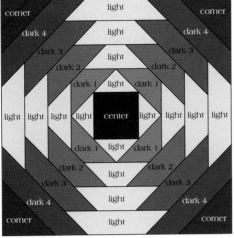

a. Center block. Make 25.

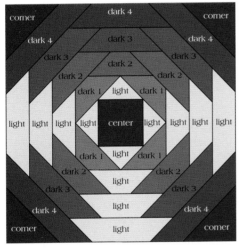

b. Side block. Make 20.

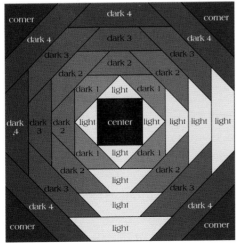

c. Corner block. Make 4.

Fig. 4–3. There are three different blocks in this quilt.

Borders

The border in this quilt was integrated into the quilt design by color and value. Using dark logs instead of light logs on the sides and corners of the perimeter blocks gives the effect of a border.

Finishing

- Layer the backing, batting, and quilt top; baste. Quilt the layers (see Quilting Options on page 118 for ideas).
- Use five 2¼" strips to bind the raw edges.

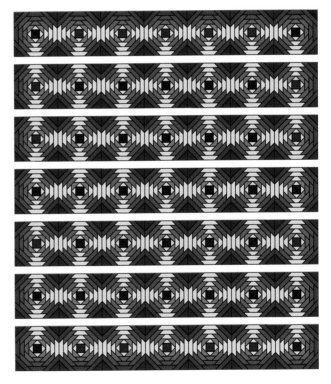

Quilt assembly

PINEAPPLE RHAPSODY

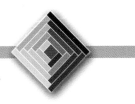

6" Pineapple Block with Four Rounds
Trim block to 6½".

Strip widths:
A – scant 1¾" square
B – generous 1⅝" square

C – generous 1" strip
D – 1¼" strip
E – 2⅝" square

Cut B and E in half on the diagonal.

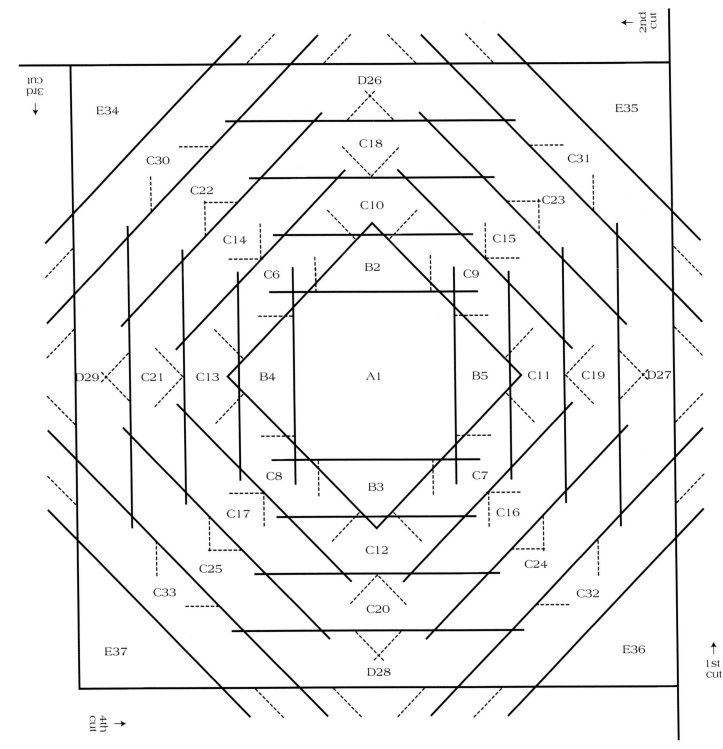

From This Day Forward

From This Day Forward, machine pieced, and machine and hand appliquéd by the author; machine quilted by Carol Seeley of Campbell River, B.C., Canada.

Finished quilt size 60" x 60"
Quilt size before borders 48½" x 48½"
Sixty-four 4" Log Cabin blocks,
   three rounds
Forty-eight 4" signature blocks
Thirty-two 2" x 4" half signature blocks

Fabric Requirements
Based on 42"-wide fabric.

Blocks
   LIGHTS: assorted fabrics to total 1¼ yards
   DARKS: assorted fabrics to total 1½ yards
   APPLIQUÉD HEARTS: ¼ yard of one fabric
   or ⅛ yard of each of four fabrics

Fabric	Yards
Signature squares, corner squares, & side rectangles	2
Log Cabin centers	⅛
Accent triangles	¾
Appliqué leaves	⅛
Inner border	¼
Outer border: cut crosswise OR	1
cut lengthwise	2
Binding	½
Backing	3¾

Cutting Instructions
• Cut strips selvage to selvage.

CENTER SQUARES: Cut two 1⅛" strips, crosscut into 1⅛" squares for a total of 64 squares.

LIGHTS: Cut one generous 1" strip and one 1¼" strip.

DARKS: Cut one generous 1" strip and one 1¼" strip.

ACCENT: Cut six 3¼" strips, crosscut into 64 – 3¼" squares. Cut each square in half diagonally to make the accent triangles.

SIGNATURE FABRIC: Cut two 2½" strips and crosscut them into four 2½" corner squares and 12 – 2½" x 4½" side rectangles.

Log Cabins and Setting Pieces
• Make 64 copies of the foundation pattern for the 4" Log Cabin block with three rounds on page 72.
• Foundation piece the 64 blocks (see Foundation Piecing, page 15).

Signature Blocks
Full-block frames:

To ensure that the guests did not write in the seam allowances, each fabric square was placed in a flip-up cardboard frame. Use the following instructions to make four frames:
• From lightweight colored cardboard, cut four 5" x 10" rectangles.
• For each rectangle, draw a horizontal line to divide the rectangle into two 5" squares.
• Divide the bottom square in half vertically and horizontally to produce four 2½" squares.
• Align the ¾" ruler mark on the paper edge of the divided square and draw a line. Repeat for the three remaining sides. Draw

A SPECIAL DAY

This quilt was made for our son Ryan and our beautiful "daughter," Brenda. I wanted to give them a cherished and lasting keepsake that would capture forever the joy of their special day. What could be more special than a wedding signature quilt?

A selection of photos from their wedding album, courtesy of photographer, Michael Moster, adds to the charm. There are many excellent books available on photo transfer if you want to include photos in your memory quilt.

The signature squares were prepared well in advance of Ryan and Brenda's big day, along with a guest checklist to make sure no one was missed. At the wedding reception, a quilt-signing table was placed near the entrance of the banquet hall. Comfortable chairs were available to encourage the guests to sit awhile and compose their thoughts. The groom's cousins were on hand to supervise the signing.

The smaller signature rectangles were perfect for young children, for guests who were reluctant to get too wordy, or for individuals who contributed to the success of the occasion, such as the photographer, wedding consultant, or florist. A signature fabric square, pen, and brief instructions were mailed to out-of-town relatives who were unable to attend the festivities.

Celebrate the next special event in your family with a memory signature quilt. It's a gift that will be treasured always.

diagonal lines in the top squares as shown in Fig. 4–4.

- With scissors or a rotary cutter, remove the arrow-shaped center section and fold the frame in half. Make four frames.
- Lay the frames on a flat surface and turn each one in a different direction. Write on each frame, "Point arrow [up, down, left, right] when signing." Be sure to point the arrow in the correct direction as you write these instructions to make the guests rotate the blocks to read the instructions (Fig. 4–5).
- To ensure that you have the same number of blocks for each direction, distribute them equally in four boxes before the reception. If you prefer, you can hand the frames out to your guests in a planned rotation or mark on a master list which way each guest signs. The last method is the one we used, and it worked fine.

Half-block frames:

The half blocks go around the edges of the quilt.

- Cut eight 3" x 10" rectangles. You will need a left-pointing frame and a right-pointing frame for each of the four directions, for a total of eight frames.
- Follow the instructions for making the whole-block frames, except mark a point ¼" beyond the midpoint on one side of the block. Draw a diagonal line from the mark to the corner, as shown in Fig. 4–6.
- Write arrow directions on the frames as you did for the whole-block frames (Fig. 4–7).

Prepare signature fabric:

- From the signature fabric, cut 48 – 5" squares for the full blocks and 32 – 3" x 5" rectangles for the half blocks. Be sure to cut a few extra squares and rectangles in case any are spoiled.

- From freezer paper, cut as many 4½" squares and 2½" x 4½" rectangles as you have fabric pieces. With a warm dry iron, press the freezer paper in the centers (wrong side) of the fabric pieces. Store them in a firm box until the big day.

- Use black .01 fabric pens to sign the blocks. It's a good idea to have two large fabric squares stabilized with freezer paper available for guests to practice on and get the feel of writing on fabric.

Sewing signature blocks:

- You may want to make two or more practice blocks to perfect the seam allowance width and block trimming before starting on the signed blocks. Choose a spoiled square or sign a square to make this practice run as realistic as possible.

- Remove the freezer paper squares and rectangles and save them for future signature quilts.

- Press the fabric squares with a warm, dry iron to set the ink.

- Slide each signature square and rectangle in the empty frames to determine which direction the block was signed.

- Open the frame and place a small "x" in each corner of the fabric square to be cut at an angle.

- Center the signature square on the paper foundation and secure it with a small dab of fabric glue. The edges of the block will extend ¼" past the pattern line on all four sides.

- Trim the two X-marked sides just inside the fabric placement lines and attach the accent triangles.

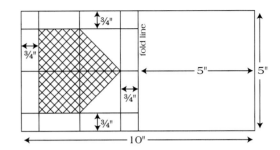

Fig. 4–4. Cardboard frame for signature blocks.

Fig. 4–5. Write signing instructions on each frame.

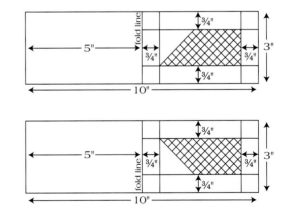

Fig. 4–6. Half-block frames.

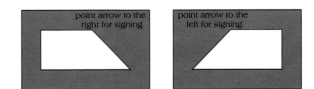

Fig. 4–7. Write signing instructions on the frames.

Trimming signature blocks:
- This block is easy to trim because there is only one point. Use the cutting extension lines on the pattern as guides. Place the ¼" ruler line just outside the point. Moving the ruler off the point will guarantee that it is not lost in the seam allowance when two blocks are sewn together.
- Make two practice blocks and sew them together point to point (see page 45 for instructions).
- Open the blocks and inspect the points. If the points are too far away from the seam allowance, you are either sewing with a scant seam allowance or the cut was too far from the point. If the point is missing, you are either sewing with a generous seam allowance or the cut was too close to the point.
- Press the seam allowances open to distribute the bulk equally on both sides of the seam and ensure that both points are sharp.
- Follow the previous instructions to make 32 half signature blocks.

TIP: I began with the blocks signed by close family members. It was less stressful knowing I could easily replace the block if I made an error. Out-of-town guests' blocks were left until last.

Quilt Assembly
- Sew the light sides of the Log Cabin blocks together in sets of four to make 16 – 8" squares.

- Use a fine-tipped permanent marker to trace the heart and leaf patterns on template plastic. Cut the designs from the template plastic and trace 16 hearts and 32 leaves on freezer paper. Appliqué the blocks.
- Join the full and half signature blocks, point to point, in pairs.
- Refer to the Quilt Assembly diagram and quilt photo for block placement. Use a ¼" foot and stitch length set at 12 stitches to the inch or 2.0 to join blocks, signature pairs, and setting pieces in rows.

TIP: Because there is a lot of bulk where the signature blocks are sewn to the Log Cabin blocks, I recommend pressing seam allowances toward the Log Cabin blocks.

- Sew the rows together. Press seam allowances toward the Log Cabin blocks.

Borders
Refer to the instructions for measuring the quilt top and adding borders (page 123).

Border 1:
- Cut six 1¼" strips from the width of the fabric. Remove the selvages from all the strips.
- Cut two strips in half and sew a half strip to each full strip. Press seam allowances open.

Outer border:
- For a border cut on the length of grain, cut four 5½" strips.

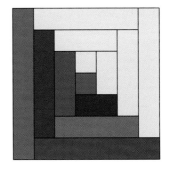

- For a border cut on the cross grain, cut six 5½" strips. Piece the strips the same way as the inner border.

Finishing

- Layer the backing, batting, and quilt top; baste. Quilt the layers (see Quilting Options on page 118 for ideas).
- Use seven 2¼" strips to bind the raw edges.

Fabric placement guides

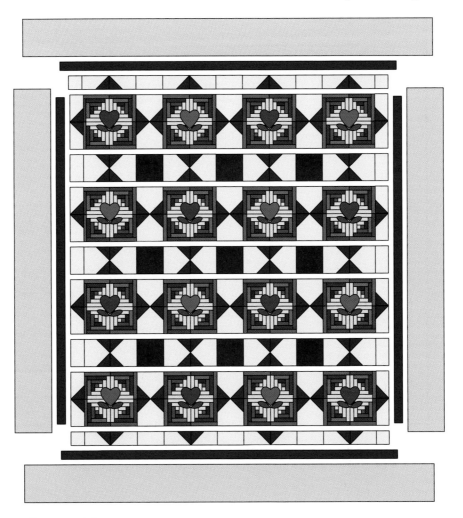

Quilt assembly

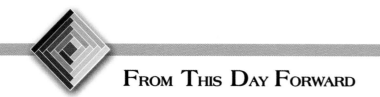

FROM THIS DAY FORWARD

Patterns may be copied for personal use.

4" Log Cabin with Three Rounds
Trim block to 4½".

Strip widths
A – 1⅛" square
B – generous 1" strip
C – 1¼" strip

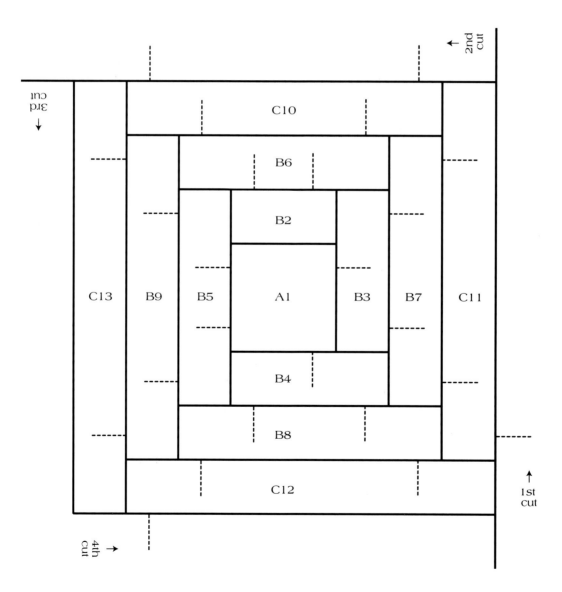

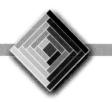

4" Signature Block

Trim block to 4½".

Strip widths

A – 5" square

B – 3¼" square cut once on the diagonal

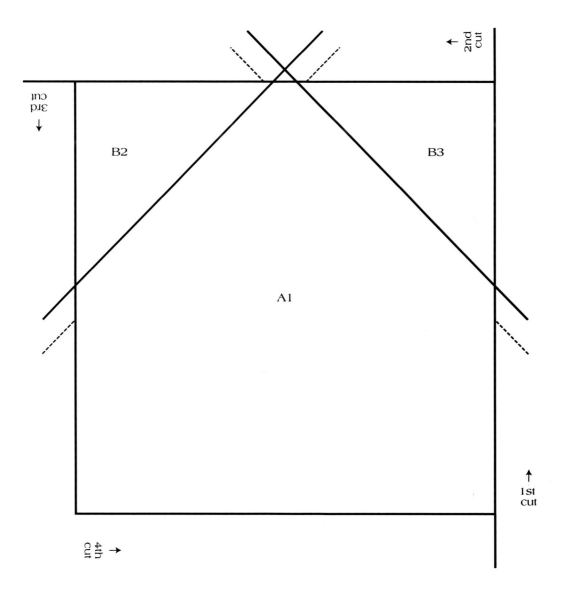

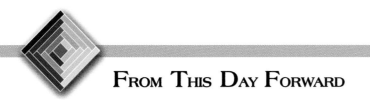

Patterns may be copied for personal use.

2" x 4" Half Signature Block

Trim block to 2½" x 4½".

Strip widths

A – 3" x 5"

B – 3¼" square cut once on the diagonal

Heart and Leaf Appliqué Pattern

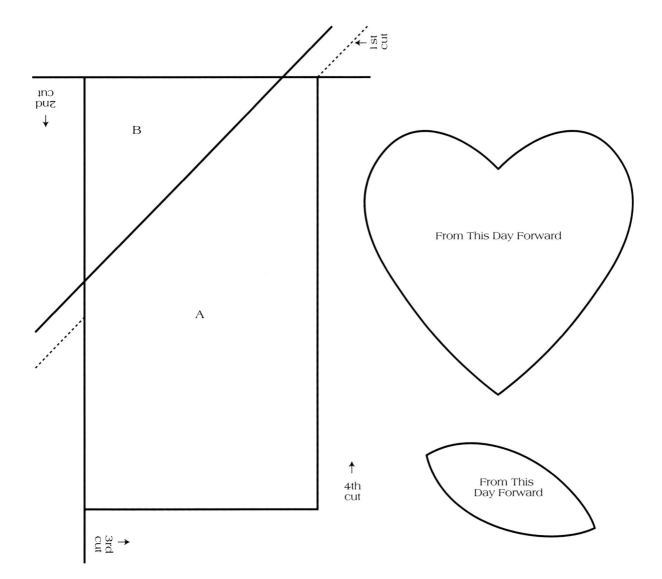

VICTORIAN TOPIARY

VICTORIAN TOPIARY, designed by the author; pieced, hand appliquéd, and machine quilted by Dorothy Housden of Surrey, B.C., Canada. The bird is by Brandywine Designs.

Finished quilt size 23½" x 43½"
Quilt size before borders 14" x 34"
Four 7" Thin and Thick blocks,
    four rounds
Four 7" Log Cabins, three rounds
One 7" modified Log Cabin, three rounds
One 7" mirror-image modified Log Cabin,
    three rounds

Fabric Requirements
Based on 42"-wide fabric.

Fabric	Yards
Floral print	¼
Light background	¾
Flowerpot	⅛
Stem	⅛
Bow	⅛
Bird	scraps
Inner border	¼
Outer border	⅝
Binding	⅓
Backing	1½

Cutting Instructions
- Cut strips selvage to selvage.
    FLORAL PRINT: Cut three 1½" B strips and two 1¾" D strips.
    STEM: Cut one 1¼" strip. From the strip, cut two 1¼" squares and four 8" pieces.
    FLOWERPOT: Cut one 1½" B strip and one 1¾" D strip. Cut two A1 squares from the 1½" B strip.
    LIGHT BACKGROUND: Cut four 1½" B strips, four 1" C strips, four 1¾" D strips, and two 1¼" E strips. Cut eight A1 squares from a 1½" B strip.

Block Assembly
Refer to the quilt photo and assembly diagrams for stem placement and block orientation.
Leaf section:
- Make four copies of the foundation pattern for the 7" Thin and Thick block with four rounds. All four blocks are identical except for the stem pieces in blocks L3 and L4.
- Use a 1½" light B square for A1. Using the floral fabric for the thick logs and the background fabric for the narrow logs, make blocks L1 and L2 (see Quilt Assembly diagram, page 78).
- Construct blocks L3 and L4 in the normal way until you get to the stem piece. Before sewing Logs E16 or E17 to the foundation, switch to a ¼" foot and sew the 1¼" stem squares to the background strips in the locations shown in Fig. 4–8. Press the seam allowances toward the background.
- Align the stem seam with the slash-marked line on the foundation. Pin the logs carefully and use a walking foot to sew them to the foundation.

Stem section:
- Make four copies of the foundation pattern for the 7" Log Cabin block with three rounds on page 80. Include the stem fabric placement line in Log C13. Note that all four blocks are identical (Fig. 4–9).
- Make blocks S1, S2, S3, and S4 in the normal way until you get to log C13. For C13, sew a 1" background strip to the block.

TIP: It's important that the stem fabric placement line be clearly visible after C13 has been added. If the line is covered, use scissors to trim the log before adding the stem.

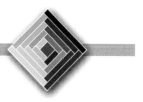

- For the stem, sew a 1¼" strip to the foundation. Be precise in sewing and trimming to be sure the stem seams will match when the blocks are joined.

Flowerpot section:

- Make one copy of the foundation pattern for the modified 7" Log Cabin block with three rounds. Make another copy that is a mirror image of this block as shown in Fig. 4–10 (see mirror-image instructions under transfer pen, page 15).
- Use 1½" dark squares, cut from a B strip, for the center squares. Construct one flowerpot block and one mirror-image block. Trim block to 7½" wide and 6½" high.

Quilt Assembly

- *To ensure a perfect stem match, sew block S1 to S3 and S2 to S4. Press the seam allowances in alternating directions, then sew the blocks together.*
- Referring to the quilt photo and quilt assembly diagram, sew the remaining blocks together in horizontal pairs. Press seam allowances in one direction in even-numbered rows. Press them in the opposite direction in odd-numbered rows. Sew the rows together.
- Decorate your Victorian Topiary with an appliquéd bow and a little bird perched on the edge of the flowerpot.

Inner Border

- Cut three strips 1¼" wide. Cut one strip in half.
- Measure the length of the quilt through the center and cut two strips this size. Pin the borders in place and sew. Press seam allowances away from the quilt top.
- Measure the width of the quilt top through the center, including side borders, and cut

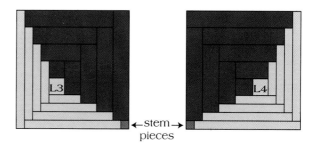

Fig. 4–8. Blocks L3 and L4 with stem pieces.

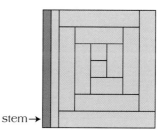

Fig. 4–9. Log Cabin block with stem.

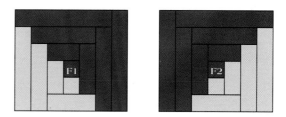

Fig. 4–10. Flowerpot blocks F1 and F2.

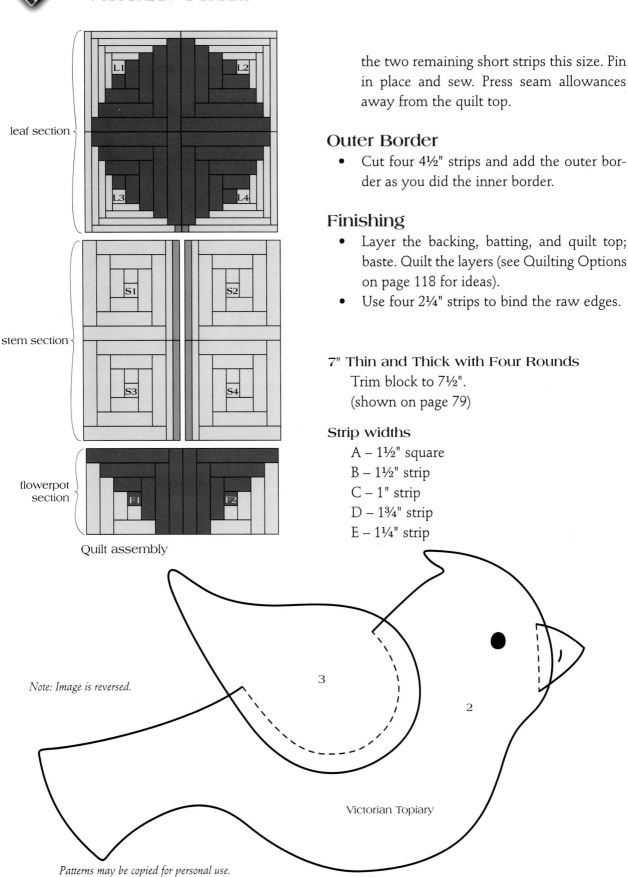

leaf section

L1 L2

L3 L4

stem section

S1 S2

S3 S4

flowerpot section

F1 F2

Quilt assembly

the two remaining short strips this size. Pin in place and sew. Press seam allowances away from the quilt top.

Outer Border

- Cut four 4½" strips and add the outer border as you did the inner border.

Finishing

- Layer the backing, batting, and quilt top; baste. Quilt the layers (see Quilting Options on page 118 for ideas).
- Use four 2¼" strips to bind the raw edges.

7" Thin and Thick with Four Rounds

Trim block to 7½".

(shown on page 79)

Strip widths

A – 1½" square
B – 1½" strip
C – 1" strip
D – 1¾" strip
E – 1¼" strip

Note: Image is reversed.

3

2

Victorian Topiary

Patterns may be copied for personal use.

7" Thin and Thick Block with 4 Rounds
(leaf section)

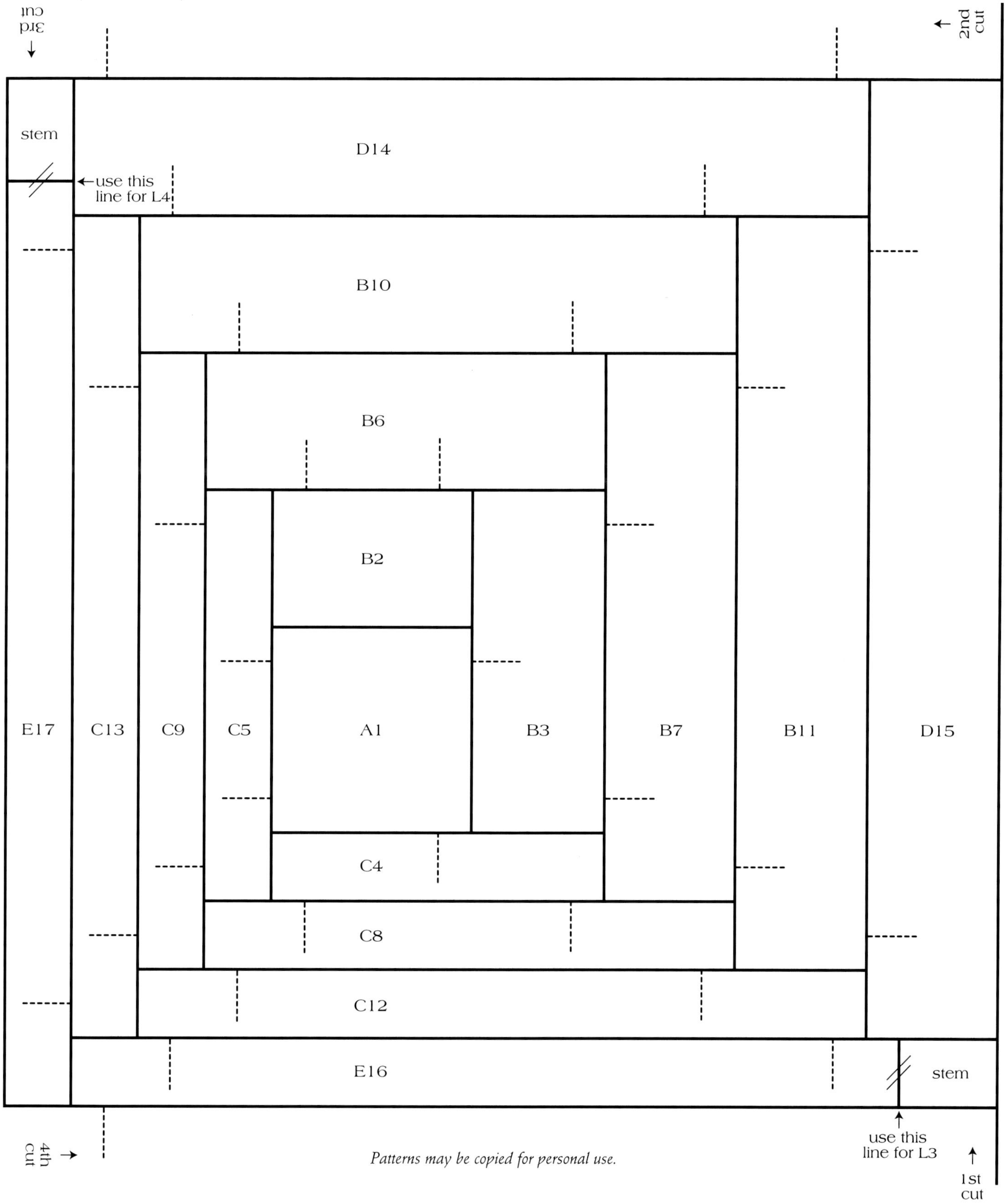

3rd cut

2nd cut

stem

D14

← use this line for L4

B10

B6

B2

A1 | B3

B7 | B11 | D15

E17 | C13 | C9 | C5

C4

C8

C12

E16

stem

use this line for L3

4th cut

1st cut

Patterns may be copied for personal use.

Victorian Topiary

7" Log Cabin Block with 3 Rounds
(stem section for Victorian Topiary &
handle for Baskets and Blooms)

Strip Widths
A – 1½" square   C – 1¼" stem/handle strip
B – 1½" strip   D – 1¾" strip
C – 1" background strip

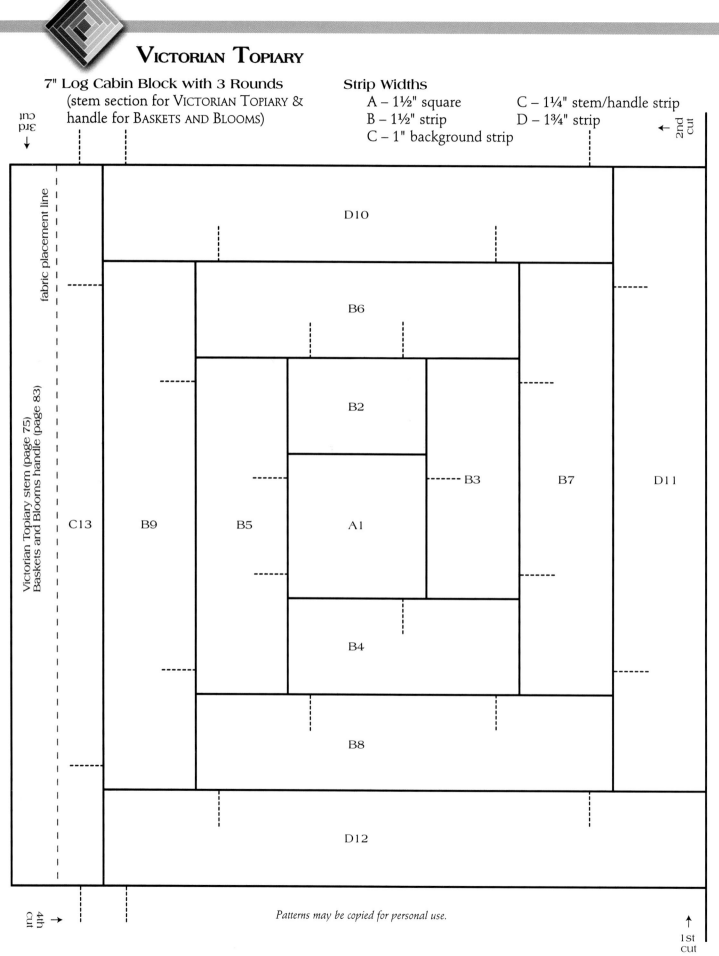

7" Modified Log Cabin with Three Rounds

(flowerpot section)

Trim block to 7½" wide x 6½" long.

Make one regular and one mirror-image foundation.

Strip widths

A – 1½" square

B – 1½" strip

C – 1¾" strip

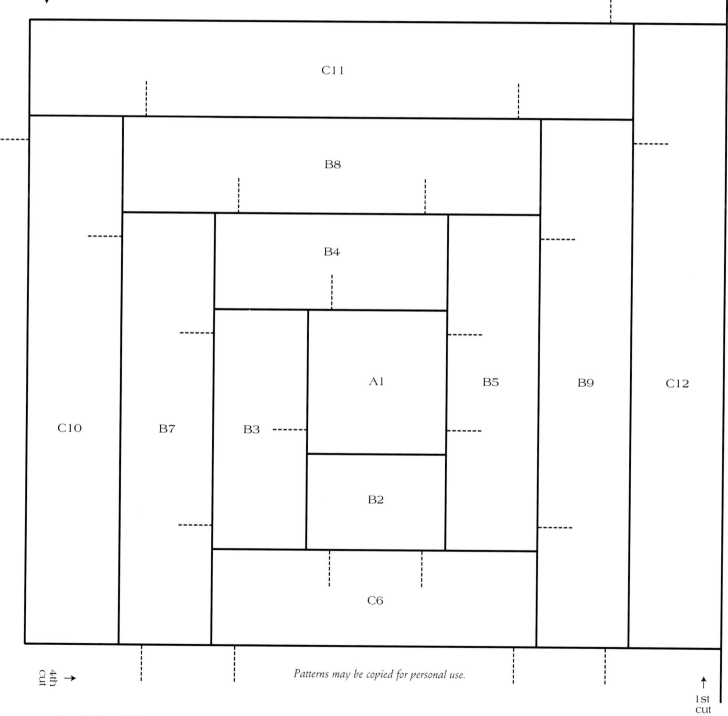

Patterns may be copied for personal use.

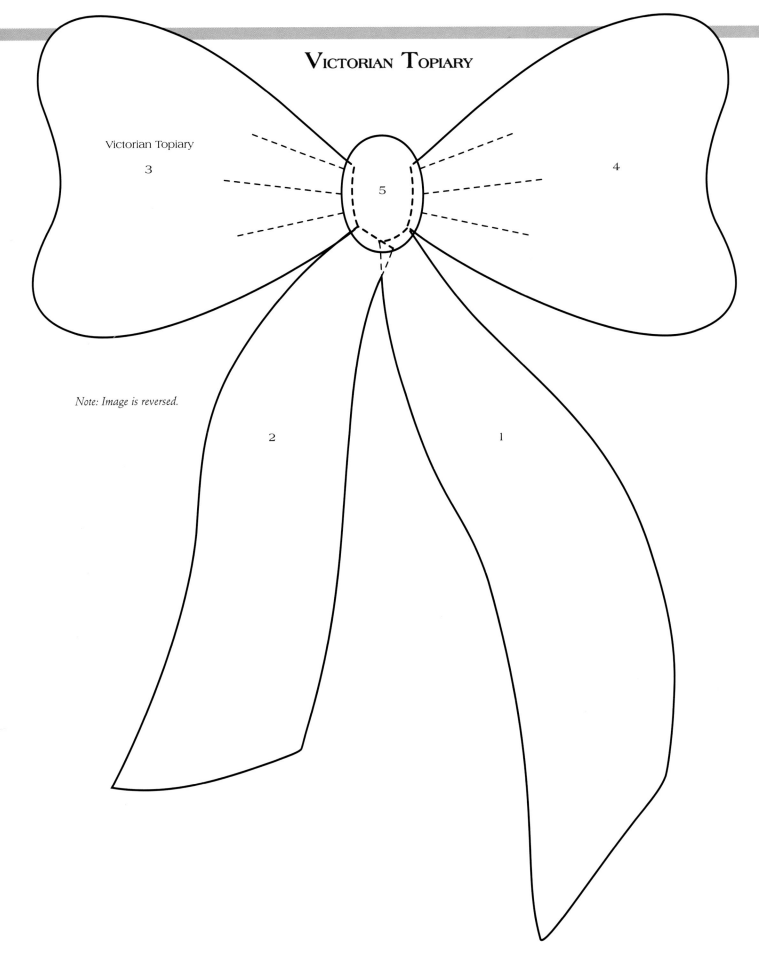

Victorian Topiary

Victorian Topiary

3

4

5

2

1

Note: Image is reversed.

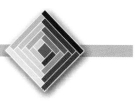

Baskets and Blooms

Baskets and Blooms, designed by the author; pieced, and machine appliquéd and machine quilted by Jean Chisholm of Surrey, B.C., Canada.

Finished quilt size 37¾" x 36¾"
Quilt size before borders 30¼" x 29¼"
Eight 7" Log Cabin blocks, three rounds
Four modified 7" x 6"
    Thin and Thick blocks
Four mirror-image modified 7" x 6"
    Thin and Thick blocks

Fabric Requirements
Based on 42"-wide fabric.

Fabric	Yards
Light background	1
Baskets	½
Flowers	scraps
Leaves	scraps
Sashing	¼
Border	⅝
Binding	⅓
Backing	1¼
Fusible web	½

Cutting Instructions
• Cut strips selvage to selvage.

BASKET: Cut one 1¼" strip for handles, three 1½" B strips, and two 1¾" D strips.

LIGHT BACKGROUND: Cut six 1½" B strips, four 1" C strips, four 1¾" D strips, two 1¼" E strips, and four 1" x 14½" strips for the top of the handle sections.

SASHING: Cut the following sashing pieces: two strips 1¼" x 14½", one strip 1¼" x 29¼", two strips 1¼" x 28¼", and two strips 1¼" x 30¾".

Handle Blocks
• Make eight copies of the foundation pattern for the 7" Log Cabin block with three rounds (page 80). Include the handle placement line in Log C13. Note that all eight blocks are identical (Fig. 4–11).
• Cut the A1 center squares from a light background 1½" B strip.
• Make the blocks in the normal way until you get to log C13. For C13, sew a 1" background strip to the foundation. Be precise in sewing and trimming to be sure the stem seams will match when the blocks are joined.

> TIP: It's important that the handle fabric placement line be clearly visible after log C13 has been added. If the line is covered, use scissors to trim the log just inside the line before adding the handle.

• For the handle, sew a 1¼" basket strip to the foundation.

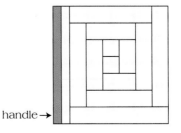

handle→

Fig. 4–11. Log Cabin block with handle.

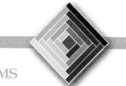

Basket Blocks

- Cut the A1 center squares from a light background 1½" B strip.
- For the left sides of the baskets, make four copies of the foundation pattern for the modified 7" Thin and Thick block. Make four mirror images of the pattern for the right side (see mirror-image instructions under transfer pen, page 15).
- Using the basket fabric for the B and D logs and the light background fabric for the C and E logs, make the four regular and four mirror-image blocks.

Quilt Assembly

- Switch to a ¼" foot for joining blocks. Press seam allowances toward the sashing.
- With the handle strips together, join two handle blocks. Repeat to make four handle sections.
- Add a 1" x 14½" strip of light background fabric to the top of each handle section (Fig. 4–12).
- Join a right and left basket block (Fig. 4–13). Make four sections like this. Press the seam allowances between blocks in the opposite direction from the handle sections.
- Sew the basket and handle sections together to make four complete baskets (Fig. 4–14).
- Refer to the Quilt Assembly diagram. Join baskets 1 and 2 with a 1¼" x 14½" sashing strip for row 1.
- Join baskets 3 and 4 with a 1¼" x 14½" sashing strip for row 2.
- Join rows 1 and 2 with a 1¼" x 29¼" sashing strip.
- Add a 1¼" x 28¼" sashing strip to each side of the quilt and a 1¼" x 30¾" sashing strip to the top and bottom.

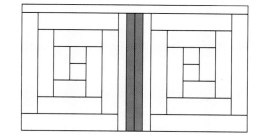

Fig. 4–12. Add a background strip at the top.

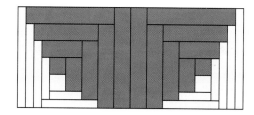

Fig. 4–13. Join left and right basket blocks.

Fig. 4–14. Join the two sections.

Quilt assembly

- The flowers and leaves are fused onto the background fabric and finished with a machine blanket stitch. Use the appliqué designs below to add colorful blooms to your Log Cabin baskets.

Borders

- Cut four 4¼" border strips. Measure the length of the quilt through the center and cut two strips this size. Pin the borders in place and sew. Press seam allowances away from the quilt top.
- Measure the width of the quilt top through the center, including side borders, and cut the two remaining strips this size. Pin in place and sew. Press seam allowances away from the quilt top.

Finishing

- Layer the backing, batting, and quilt top; baste. Quilt the layers. See Quilting Options, page 118, for quilting ideas.
- Use seven 2¼" strips to bind the raw edges.

Patterns may be copied for personal use.

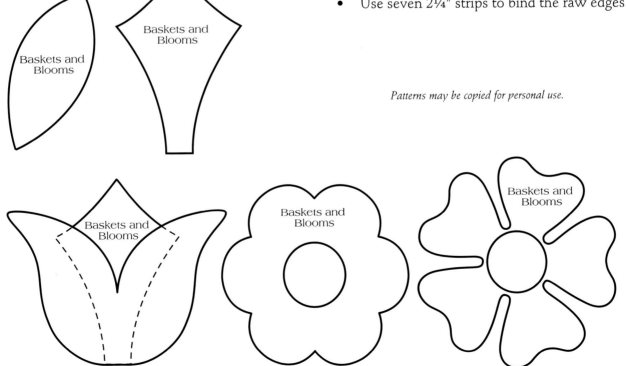

Baskets and Blooms

Baskets and Blooms

Baskets and Blooms

Baskets and Blooms

Baskets and Blooms

Baskets and Blooms

BASKETS AND BLOOMS

7" modified Log Cabin with Three Rounds
Trim block to 7½" wide x 6½" long.

Strip widths
A – 1½" square
B – 1½" strip
C – 1" strip
D – 1¾" strip
E – 1¼" strip

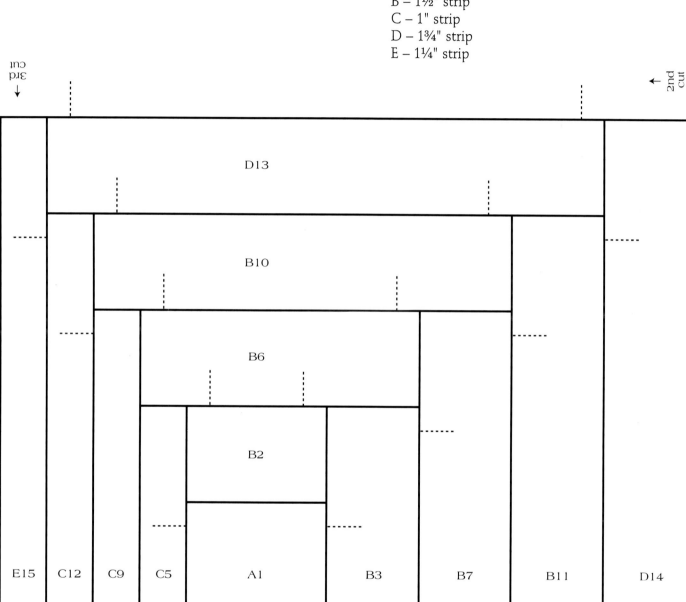

DOUBLE DELIGHT

DOUBLE DELIGHT, pieced by the author and machine quilted by
Carol Seeley of Campbell River, B.C., Canada.

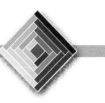
Finished quilt size 49½" x 60½"
Quilt size before borders 44" x 55"
Eighty 5½" Log Cabin blocks,
    three rounds
Seventy-six 2¾" Square-in-a-Square blocks

Fabric Requirements
Based on 42"-wide fabric.

Blocks and border:
  lights:
      assorted fabrics to total 2¾ yards
  color 1:
      assorted fabrics to total 1½ yards
  color 2:
      assorted fabrics to total 1½ yards

Binding   ½
Backing:
    crosswise seam   3¼
    OR lengthwise   3⅞

Cutting Instructions
- Cut strips selvage to selvage.
- Log Cabin: Cut one 1¼" B strip and one 1½" C strip from each fabric. Cut more strips as needed.

Square-in-a-Square:
- Cut 38 generous 2⅜" color-1 center squares (A1).
- Cut 38 generous 2⅜" color-2 center squares (A1).
- Cut 11 – 2⅝" light-colored strips and cross-cut them into 2⅝" squares. You will need a total of 152 squares. Cut each square in half on the diagonal for the B triangles.

Quilt Assembly
- Make 80 copies of the 5½" Log Cabin block with three rounds on page 91.
- Make 76 copies of the 2¾" Square-in-a-Square block on page 92. (Two of these blocks will fit on a page for copying.)
- To begin the Log Cabin block, scissor-cut a 1½" square from any of the dark C strips for A1. For added interest, use a variety of fabrics for the center squares.
- Construct 40 color-1 and 40 color-2 Log Cabin blocks (refer to Foundation Piecing, page 15).
- Make 76 Square-in-a-Square blocks (see page 44).

Off-Center Barn Raising setting
- Refer to the Quilt Assembly diagram, page 58, and quilt photo for block placement. Use a ¼" foot and stitch length set at 12 stitches to the inch or 2.0 to join blocks in 10 rows of eight each.
- Press seam allowances in one direction in even-numbered rows and in the opposite direction in odd-numbered rows.
- Sew the rows together. Press seam allowances downward between rows.

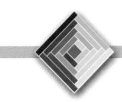

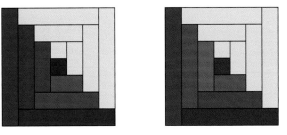

Fabric placement guide for Log Cabin

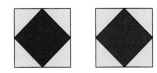

Fabric placement guide for Square-in-a-Square

Quilt assembly

Borders

- **LEFT BORDER:** Starting with a Color-1 Square-in-a-Square block and alternating colors, sew 20 blocks together. Press the seam allowances upward, opposite the direction from the quilt top.
- **RIGHT BORDER:** Starting with a Color-2 block and alternating colors, sew 20 blocks together. Press the seam allowances upward.
- **TOP BORDER:** Starting with a Color-2 block, sew 18 blocks together. Press seams allowances in the opposite direction from top row of the quilt.
- **BOTTOM BORDER:** Starting with a Color-1 block, sew 18 blocks together. Press the seam allowances in the opposite direction from the bottom row of the quilt.
- Add the borders to the quilt top in the same order they were made. For the left border, position the Color-1 square in the top corner. Position the Color-2 square at the top on the right row. Pin in place and sew. Press seam allowances away from the quilt top.

Finishing

- Layer the backing, batting, and quilt top; baste. Quilt the layers (see Quilting Options on page 118 for ideas).
- Use six 2¼" strips to bind the raw edges.

DOUBLE DELIGHT

5½" Log Cabin with Three Rounds
Trim block to 6".

Strip widths
A – 1½" square
B – 1¼" strip
C – 1½" strip

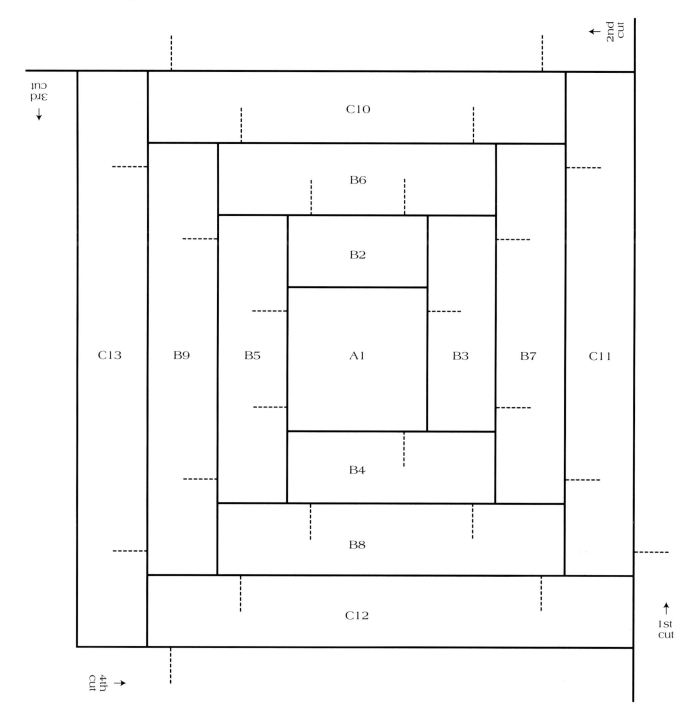

2¾" Square-in-a-Square

Trim block to 3¼".

Strip widths

A – generous 2⅜" square

B – 2⅝" square

Cut B squares in half on the diagonal.

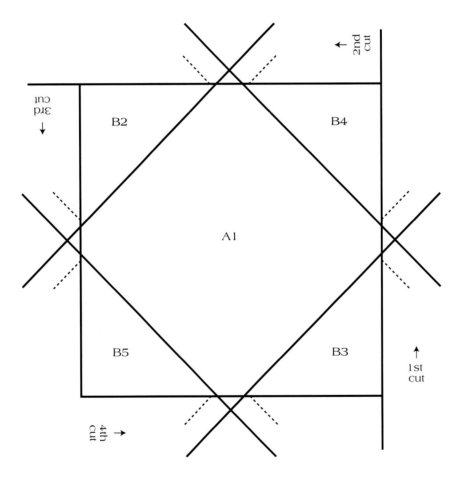

CRYSTAL CABINS

CRYSTAL CABINS, pieced and machine quilted by Val Smith of White Rock, B.C., Canada.

Finished quilt size 58" x 80"
Quilt size before borders 44" x 66"
Ninety-six 5½" Log Cabin blocks,
  three rounds

Fabric Requirements
Based on 42"-wide fabric.

Blocks and pieced borders:
  assorted lights to total 2½ yards
  assorted mediums to total 2¼ yards
  assorted darks to total 1¼ yards

Fabric	Yards
Dark border	
and binding	2¼
Backing:	
crosswise seam	3⅝
OR lengthwise	4⅞

Cutting Instructions

Cut strips selvage to selvage. Cut one 1¼" B strip and one 1½" C strip from all the light, medium, and dark fabrics.

Quilt Assembly
- Make 96 copies of the 5½" Log Cabin blocks with three rounds on page 91.
- Scissor-cut a 1½" square from any of the 1½" medium or dark C strips for A1. For added interest, use a variety of fabrics for the center squares. Cut log strips the widths given with the pattern.

- Foundation piece 64 light/medium Log Cabin blocks and 32 light/dark blocks (see Foundation Piecing, page 15).
- Refer to the Quilt Assembly diagram and quilt photo for block placement. Use a ¼" foot and stitch length set at 12 stitches to the inch or 2.0 to join blocks in 12 rows of eight each.
- Press seam allowances in one direction in even-numbered rows and in the opposite direction in odd-numbered rows.
- Sew the rows together. Press seam allowances downward between rows.

Borders
- Cut strips selvage to selvage. From the dark border fabric, cut six 1" strips, 12 – 1¼" strips, and 13 – 2½" strips.
- Re-cut the six 1" strips into 1" squares.
- For the mini-log pieced borders, cut 1" strips from a variety of dark, medium, and light fabrics. Trim leftover strips from the blocks to 1" wide. Cut the strips into varying lengths, ranging from 2" to 4½". Alternate the mini-logs with the 1" squares as you construct the borders.

There are seven border rows in this quilt, and the rows are added one at a time, starting with the side borders. Piece border strips as needed to create the required lengths. Press all seam allowances toward the outside.
- FIRST ROW: Sew 2½" dark border strips to all four sides.
- SECOND ROW: Place dark mini-logs in a pleasing arrangement, starting and ending with a dark square. Sew to the quilt.
- THIRD ROW: Add a 1¼" dark border strip to all four sides. Re-cut the short ends into 1" squares as needed.

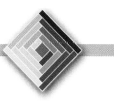

- **FOURTH ROW:** Use the medium Log Cabin fabrics to make four mini-log borders. Start and end with a 1" dark square.
- **FIFTH ROW:** Add a 1¼" dark border strip to all four sides.
- **SIXTH ROW:** Use the light Log Cabin fabrics to make four mini-log borders. Start and end with a 1" dark square.

- **SEVENTH ROW:** Add a 2½" dark strip to all four sides.

Finishing

- Layer the backing, batting, and quilt top; baste. Quilt the layers (see Quilting Options on page 118 for ideas).
- Use seven 2¼" strips to bind the raw edges.

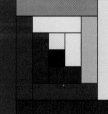

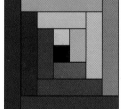

Fabric placement guide
for Log Cabin

Quilt assembly

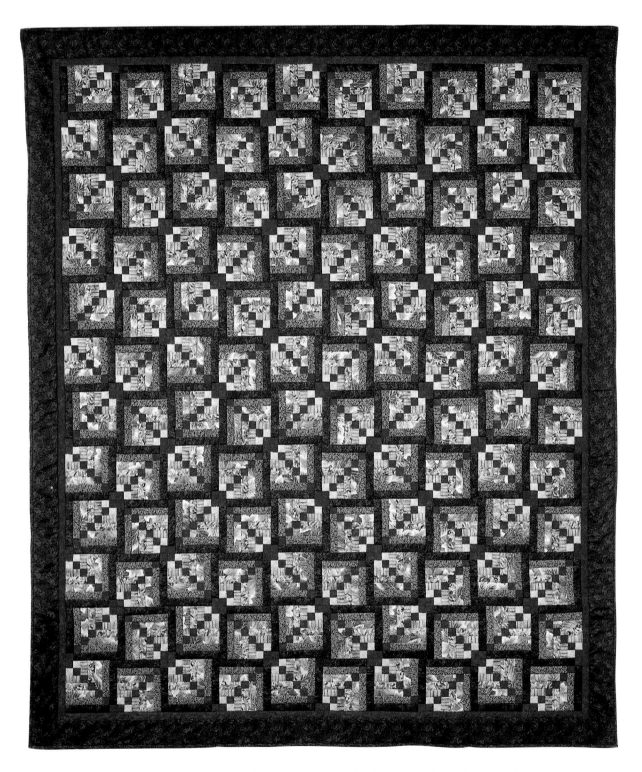

COBBLESTONES, pieced and machine quilted by Brenda Ambeault of Edmonton, AB, Canada.

Finished quilt size 80" x 94"
Quilt size before borders 70" x 84"
120 – 7" Steps to the Cabin blocks

Fabric Requirements
Based on 42"-wide fabric.

For a block with a light side and a dark side, halve the yardage requirements for each round.

Fabric	Yards
Step squares	1⅞
Inner border	½
Binding	⅔
First round	⅝
Second round	1
Third round	1¼
Fourth round	1½
Fifth round	1¾
Sixth round	2¼
Outer border:	
cut crosswise	1¼
OR lengthwise	2⅝
Backing:	
crosswise seam	5
OR lengthwise	5¾

Cutting Instructions
- Cut strips selvage to selvage.
- A SQUARES: Cut 12 – 1¾" strips. Cut six of the strips into 120 – 1¾" squares. Sew the remaining six strips to six 6¾" D strips along their length.
- C SQUARES: Cut 25 – 1½" strips for strip piecing.

Strip Piecing
Use the following measurements for strip piecing C squares and logs:

Log	Strip width	Segments
B3	1¾"	1½"
B5	2¾"	1½"
B7	3¾"	1½"
B9	4¾"	1½"
B11	5¾"	1½"
D13	6¾"	1¾"

- Cut five strips of each B fabric and six D strips.

Pre-cut Logs
The remaining logs can be cut to size as you sew or pre-cut to the following individual lengths:

Log	Strip width	Segments
B2	1½"	1¾"
B4	1½"	2¾"
B6	1½"	3¾"
B8	1½"	4¾"
B10	1½"	5¾"
D12	1¾"	6¾"

Quilt Assembly
- Make 120 copies of the 7" Steps to the Cabin block.
- Use strip piecing to sew a 1½" C strip to logs B3, B5, B7, B9, B11. Sew a 1¾" A strip to D13.

COBBLESTONES

- Foundation piece the 120 Steps to the Cabin blocks (see Foundation Piecing on pages 15 and 33).
- Refer to the Quilt Assembly diagram and quilt photo for block placement. Use a ¼" foot and stitch length set at 12 stitches to the inch or 2.0 to join blocks in 12 rows of 10 each.
- Press seam allowances in one direction in even-numbered rows and in the opposite direction in odd-numbered rows.
- Sew the rows together. Press seam allowances downward between rows.

Inner border
- Cut eight 1½" strips from the width of the fabric.
- Remove the selvages from the strips and sew them together in pairs. Press seam allowances open.
- Measure the length of the quilt through the center and cut two strips this size. Pin in place and sew. Press seam allowances away from the quilt top.
- Measure the width of the quilt through the center, including the side borders, and cut the two remaining strips this size. Pin in place and sew. Press seam allowances away from the quilt top.

Outer border
- For borders cut on the length of grain, cut four 4½" strips.
- For borders cut on the cross grain, cut eight 4½" strips. Remove the selvages and sew the strips together in pairs. Press seam allowances open.
- Add the outer borders the same way as the inner borders.

Finishing
- Layer the backing, batting, and quilt top; baste. Quilt the layers (see Quilting Options on page 118 for ideas).
- Use nine 2¼" strips to bind the raw edges.

7" Steps to the Cabin
Trim block to 7½".
(pattern on page 100)

Strip widths
A – 1¾" square
B – 1½" strip
C – 1½" square
D – 1¾" strip
Piece the C step squares to logs B3, B5, B7, B9, B11, and an A step square to D13 and attach as one unit to the foundation.

> **TIP:** The 7" Steps to the Cabin is a very versatile block. It is easily adapted to a 4", 5", or 6" Steps to the Cabin. Simply eliminate the appropriate number of outside logs and omit the step square for 4", 5", 6", and 7" Off-Center blocks.

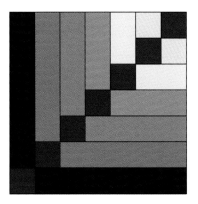

Fabric placement guide

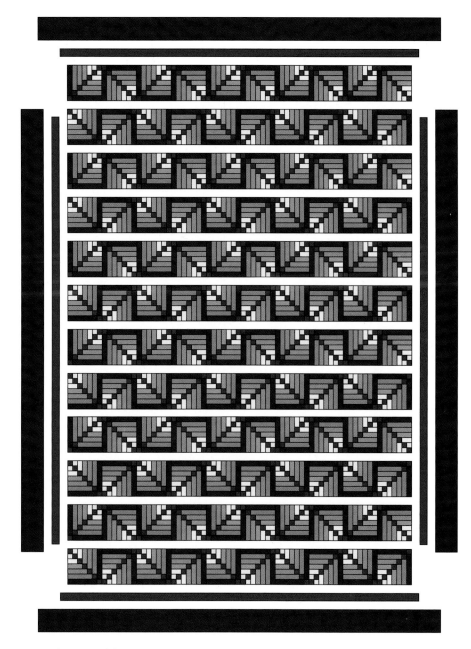

Quilt assembly

Patterns may be copied for personal use.

7" Steps to the Cabin

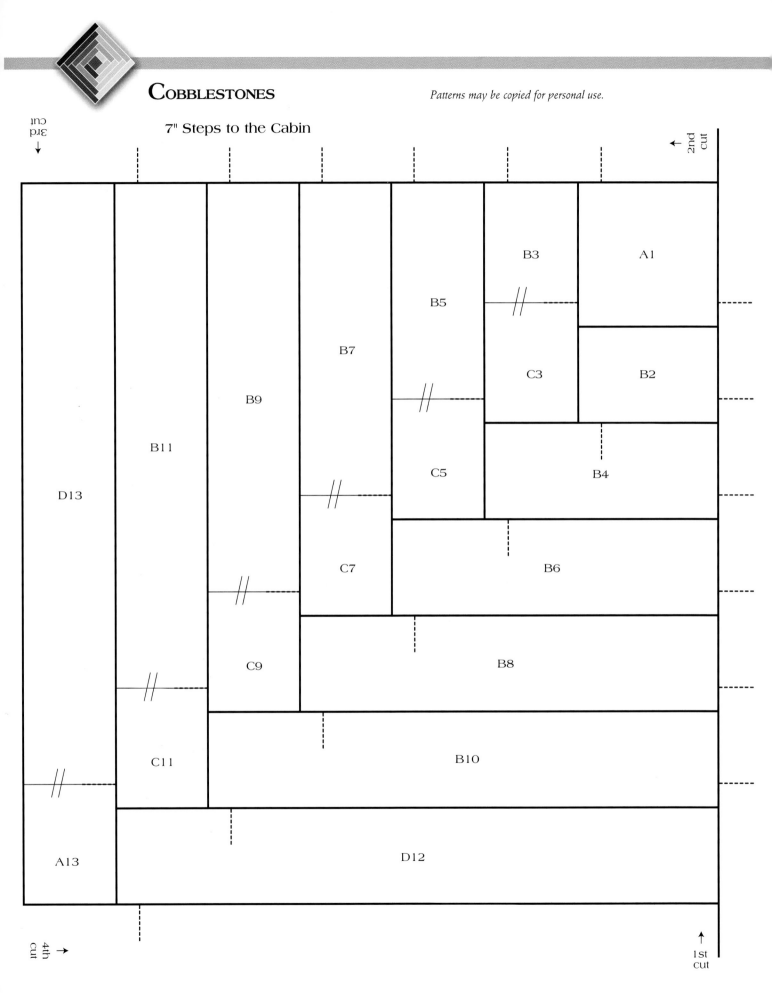

LOG CABIN REDISCOVERED BY MACHINE – Brenda Brayfield

PATCHWORK ECLIPSE

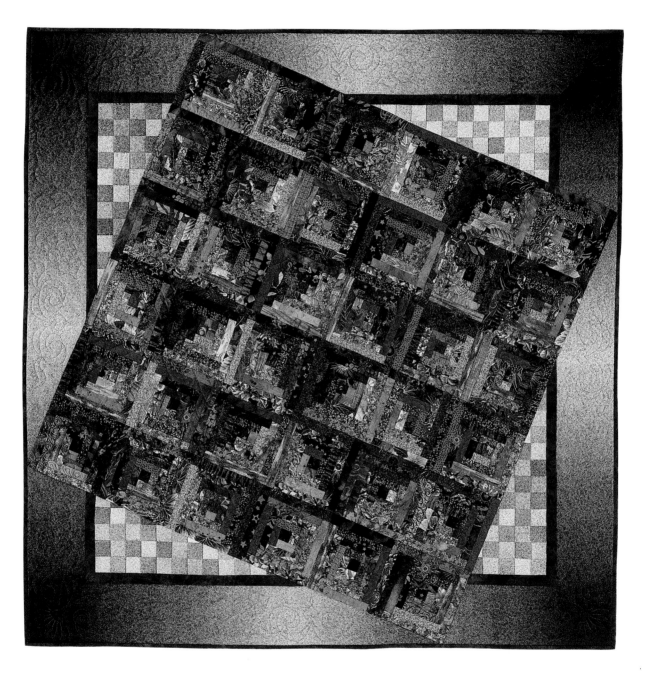

PATCHWORK ECLIPSE, pieced by the author and machine quilted by
Carol Seeley of Campbell River, B.C., Canada.

Finished quilt size 55" x 55"
Quilt size before borders 42" x 42"
Thirty-six 7" Log Cabin blocks,
     four rounds

Fabric Requirements

Based on 42"-wide fabric.

Light logs:
     assorted fabrics to total 1⅓ yards.
Dark logs and center squares:
     assorted fabrics to total 1¾ yards.
Patchwork border:
     assorted fabrics to total ½ yard, or if you
     prefer a plain corner, you will need ½
     yard of one fabric.

Fabric	Yards
Inner border	⅓
Outer border*	1⅛
Binding	½
Backing	3½
Freezer paper	1¼

*Purchase 2 yards for a gradated border.

Cutting Instructions

- Cut strips selvage to selvage. Cut one 1¼" B strip and one 1½" C strip from all the light and all the dark block fabrics.

Quilt Assembly

- Make 36 copies of the 7" Log Cabin block with four rounds on page 106.
- Scissor-cut 1½" squares from any of the 1½" dark C strips for the A1 center squares.
- Foundation piece the 36 blocks (see Foundation Piecing, page 15).

Valleys and Mountains Setting

- Refer to the Quilt Assembly diagram and quilt photo for block placement. Use a ¼" foot and stitch length set at 12 stitches to the inch or 2.0 to join blocks in six rows of six each.
- Press seam allowances in one direction in even-numbered rows and in the opposite direction in odd-numbered rows.
- Sew the rows together. Press the seam allowances downward between rows.

Borders

   This complicated-looking border is straightforward and simple to construct. Honest!

- PATCHWORK CORNER: Cut 136 2" squares. (If you prefer a plain corner, cut four 8" x 19" rectangles, one for each corner.) Use the following directions for adding borders and making a corner template.
- INNER BORDER: Cut six 1½" strips from the width of the fabric. Remove the selvages from the strips and cut two of the strips in half.
- OUTER BORDER: Cut six 6" strips from the width of the fabric. Remove the selvages from the strips and cut two of the strips in half.
- Refer to the patchwork corner guide to assemble the corner (Fig. 4–15). Place the 2" squares in a pleasing arrangement and piece them in horizontal rows, then sew the rows together. Make four patchwork corners.
- Sew a long inner and a long outer border strip together lengthwise and press seam allowances toward the outside edge. Repeat for the other three pairs.

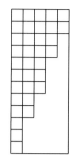

- Sew the short pairs of strips together in the same way.
- Attach a long and a short pieced border to each patchwork or plain corner. Miter the corner (Fig. 4–16). Repeat for the three remaining corners.

Corner template

Please read these instructions before proceeding. There are three important steps in italic.

- Tape the freezer paper to a large flat surface, shiny side down.
- Place a large square ruler near the top-left corner of the freezer paper. Draw an accurate 90-degree angle. Extend the top line until it measures 16" from the corner and extend the other line until it measures 39". Be exact and straight in the measuring and drawing.
- Connect the 16" mark and the 39" mark with a diagonal line (Fig. 4–17). Highlight the diagonal line to remind yourself to cut the fabric ¼" beyond the freezer paper edge.
- Slide the cutting mat under the freezer paper and, using a 6" x 24" ruler, rotary cut the triangle template on the drawn lines.
- Place a folded bed sheet, large enough to accommodate the template, on a flat surface. Place a pieced border unit on the bed sheet *right side up*. The freezer paper template is a true image, not a reversed image, and all four border sections are alike.
- Place a large square ruler on the mitered corner and check that it is 90 degrees. Place the template shiny side down on top of the border, with the *freezer paper edge ¼" away from the top and side fabric edges*.
- Lightly press the freezer paper along the top and side edges to secure it to the pieced border corner or a plain rectangle. Pressing with

Fig. 4–15. Patchwork corner guide.

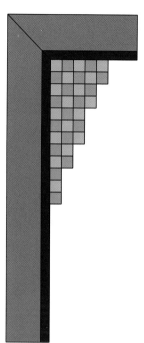

Fig. 4–16. Patchwork corner fully assembled and ready for trimming.

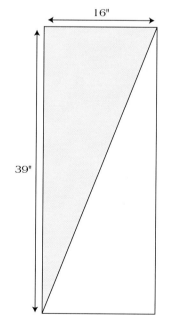

Fig. 4–17. Connect the 16" and 39" marks with a diagonal line.

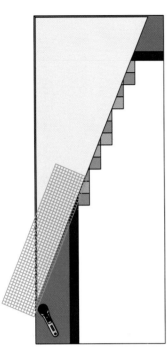

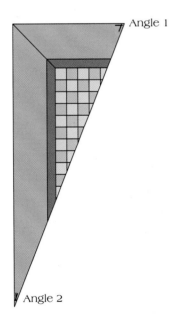

Fig. 4–18. Be sure to leave a ¼" seam allowance around all three sides of the freezer paper template.

Angle 1

Angle 2

Fig. 4–19. Mark seam intersections.

an up-and-down motion and working from the edge to the middle, secure the freezer paper to the border. Don't press too hard or for too long. The removal of a firmly secured freezer paper template could distort the long bias edge.

- Slide the cutting mat underneath the diagonal side. This is the only side to be cut. *Place the ¼" mark of a 6" x 24" ruler on the diagonal freezer paper edge and cut* (Fig. 4–18).

- Starting at the square corner, carefully remove the template. Using the same template, repeat this procedure for the remaining three border corners.

- To attach the border corners, on the wrong side of the quilt top, mark a dot in the corner ¼" in from both quilt edges.

- To mark the angles on the border section, place the ¼" line of a clear ruler on the fabric edge. Draw a short line to represent the seam line at Angle 1. Rotate the quilt and repeat on the adjacent side. Mark Angle 2 in the same way (Fig. 4–19). Mark the remaining border corners.

- Lay the quilt on a flat surface. Match the point of the two intersecting lines on Angles 1 and 2 with the appropriate marks on the quilt. Pin.

- Sew from edge to edge. Press seam allowances toward the border or press them toward the quilt if the patchwork seams lie flatter in that direction.

- Attach the three remaining border sections.

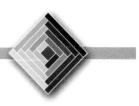

Finishing

- Layer the backing, batting, and quilt top; baste. Quilt the layers (see Quilting Options on page 118 for ideas).
- Use six 2¼" strips to bind the raw edges.

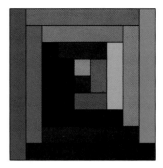

Fabric placement guide

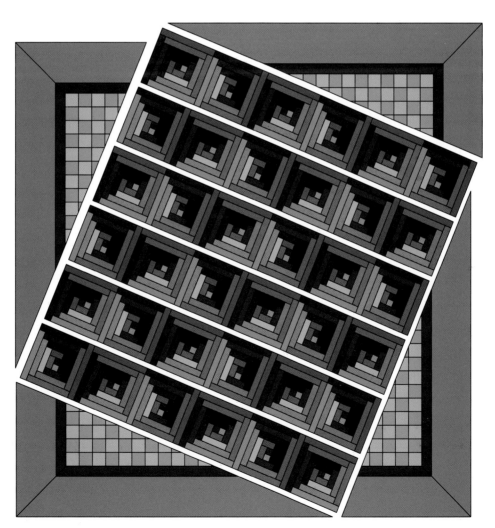

Quilt assembly

Patterns may be copied for personal use.

7" Log Cabin Block with Four Rounds
Trim block to 7½".
Also used for AUTUMN JEWELS

Strip widths
A – 1½" square
B – 1¼" strip
C – 1½" strip

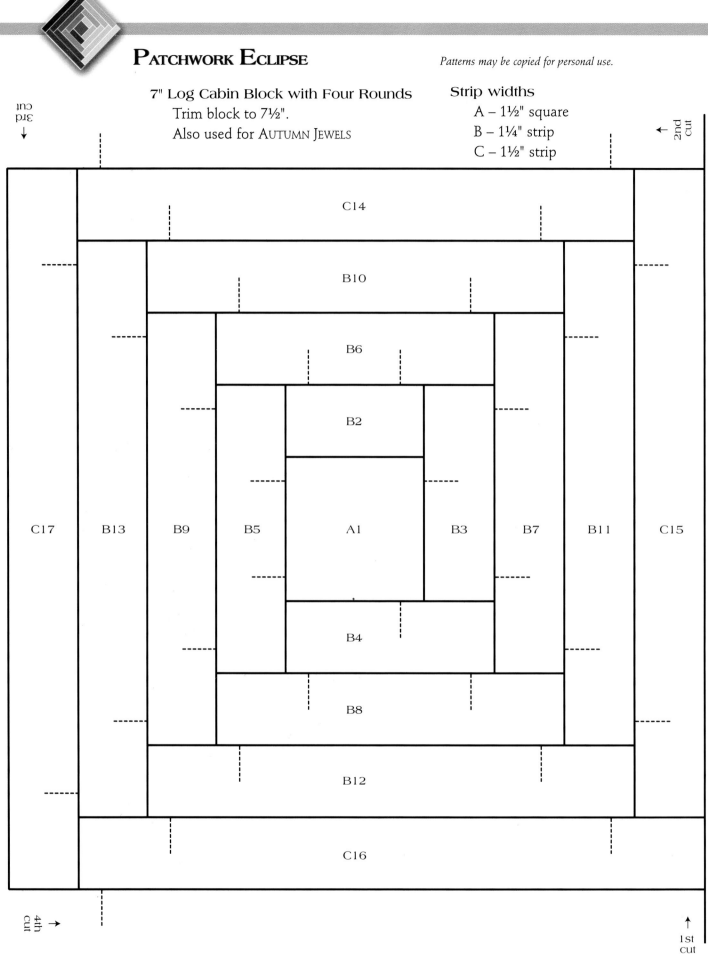

AUTUMN JEWELS, pieced by the author and machine quilted by Carol
Seeley of Campbell River, B.C., Canada.

Finished quilt size 53" x 67"
Quilt size before borders 42" x 56"
Forty-eight 7" Log Cabin blocks,
    four rounds, page 106
Two 4½" Off-Center blocks
Two 4½" mirror-image Off-Center blocks

Fabric Requirements
Based on 42"-wide fabric.

Blocks and piano-key border:
    assorted darks to total 3¼ yards
    assorted lights to total 1¾ yards

Fabric	Yards
Inner border	⅓
Binding	½
Backing	3½
crosswise	3⅜
OR lengthwise	4⅛

Cutting Instructions
- Cut one 1¼" B strip and one 1½" C strip, selvage to selvage, from all the light and all the dark fabrics.

Quilt Assembly
- Make 48 copies of the 7" Log Cabin block with four rounds on page 106.
- Make two copies of the 4½" Off-Center block and two mirror-image copies on page 110 (see mirror-image instructions under transfer pen, page 15).
- To begin a Log Cabin block, scissor-cut a 1½" square from any of the 1½" dark C strips for A1. For added interest, use a variety of fabrics for the center squares.
- Foundation piece the 48 Log Cabin blocks and the four Off-Center blocks (see Foundation Piecing, page 15).

Sunshine and Shadows setting
- Refer to the Quilt Assembly diagram and quilt photo for block placement. Use a ¼" foot and stitch length set at 12 stitches to the inch or 2.0 to join blocks in eight rows of six each.
- Press seam allowances in one direction in even-numbered rows and in the opposite direction in odd-numbered rows.
- Sew the rows together. Press seam allowances downward between rows.

Inner border
Because the width of the quilt top is 42½", the top and bottom borders will not have to be pieced if they are added before the side borders.
- Cut five 1½" strips. (If the fabric is less than 42½" wide, cut six strips and piece the top and bottom borders.)
- Measure the width of the quilt through the center and trim two strips to this size. Sew top and bottom borders to the quilt and press seam allowances away from the quilt top.
- Cut one of the three border strips in half and sew a half strip to each remaining full strip. Press seam allowances open.
- Sew the side borders to the quilt as you did for the top and bottom.

Piano-key border
- Refer to Piano-Key Border on page 117. Cut strips 1¼". Cut piano-key borders 5" wide.
- Add the side borders to the quilt. Press seam allowances toward the inner border.

- Refer to the quilt photo for accurate block placement. Sew the Off-Center blocks to the ends of the top and bottom borders and add these borders to the quilt. Press seam allowances toward the inner border.

Finishing

- Layer the backing, batting, and quilt top; baste. Quilt the layers (see Quilting Options on page 118 for ideas).
- Use seven 2¼" strips to bind the raw edges.

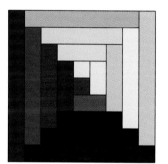

Fabric placement guide for Log Cabin

Fabric placement guide for corners

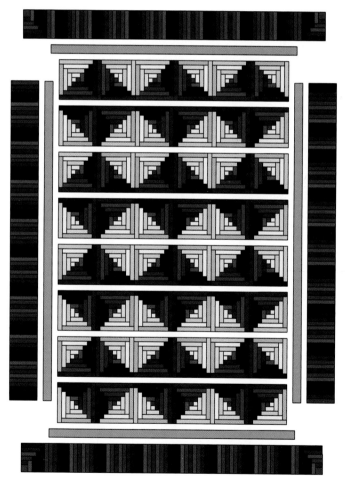

Quilt assembly

AUTUMN JEWELS

7" Log Cabin with Four Rounds
Trim block to 7½".
(shown on page 106)

Strip widths
A – 1½" square
B – 1¼" strip
C – 1½" strip
Eliminate two rounds of logs for a 4" block.

4½" Off-Center Block
Trim block to 5".
(shown below)

Strip widths
A – 1½"
B – 1¼"
C – 1½"

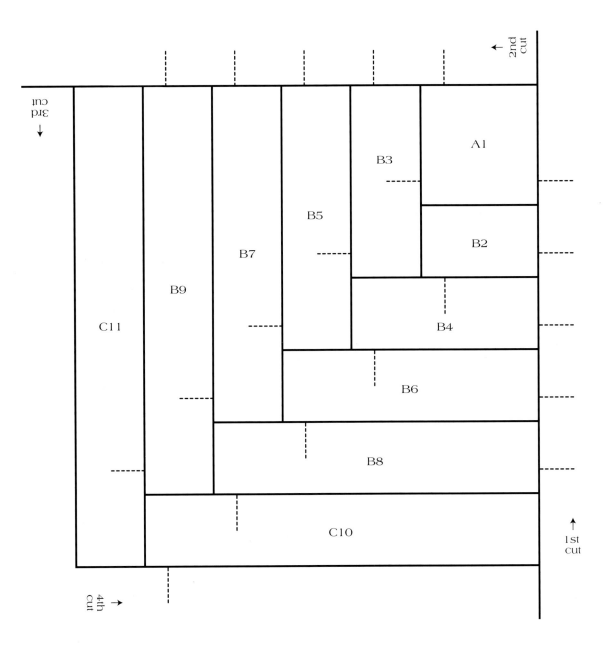

Chapter 5

Planning Your Quilt

In this section, you will find a few more Log Cabin block variations. You will also find some ideas for arranging blocks and for using blocks in borders. Quilting ideas are presented on page 118.

More Blocks

If you don't find the size block you want in this book, you can enlarge many of the blocks by adding another round of logs. To decrease the size, trace the block, omitting the outside round. Transfer the cutting and sewing extension lines to the new foundation.

Square-in-a-Square

This block is quite versatile and offers a variety of design options:

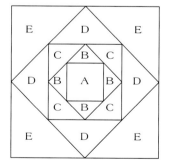

Square-in-a-Square

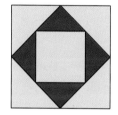

Double Square-in-a-Square: Omit A and B and use a 3" square for C.

Snail's Trail: Use a four-patch for A and alternate light and dark values within each round.

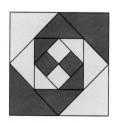

Monkey Wrench: Omit A and use a four-patch for B.

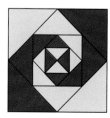

Nautilus: Use four quarter-square triangles for A.

6" Square-in-a-Square

Trim block to 6½".

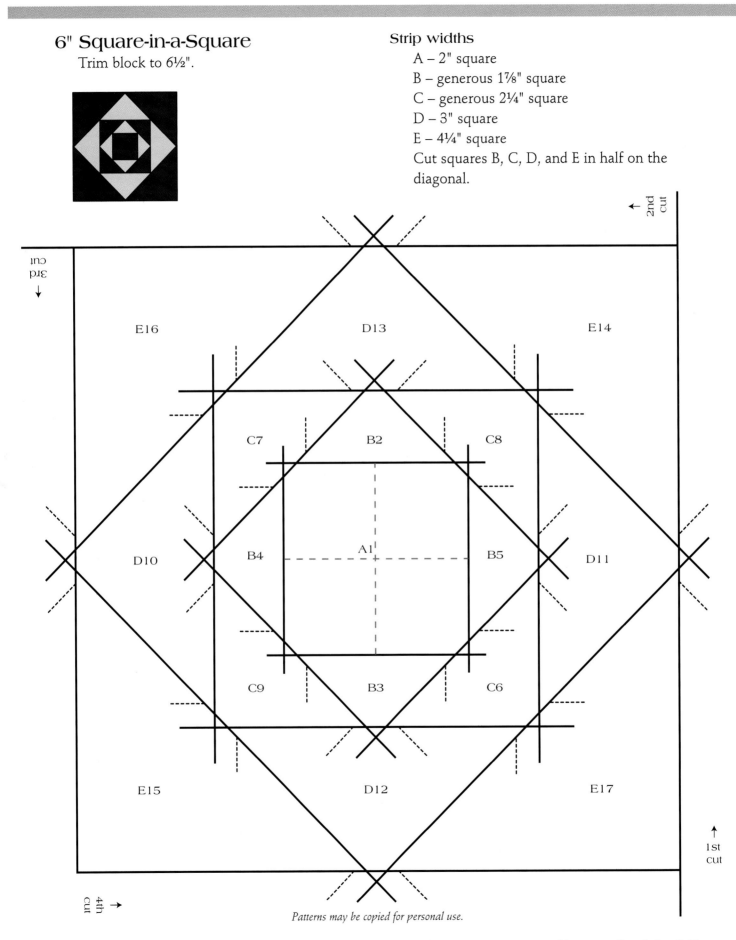

Strip widths

A – 2" square
B – generous 1⅞" square
C – generous 2¼" square
D – 3" square
E – 4¼" square

Cut squares B, C, D, and E in half on the diagonal.

2nd cut

3rd cut

E16   D13   E14

C7   B2   C8

D10   B4   A1   B5   D11

C9   B3   C6

E15   D12   E17

1st cut

4th cut

Patterns may be copied for personal use.

Strip widths

Center – 2½" square
A – 1¼" strip
B – generous 1⅛" strip
C – 1⅛" strip
D – 1⅜" strip
E – 3⅜" square (2)

6" Pineapple with 3 Rounds

Trim block to 6½".

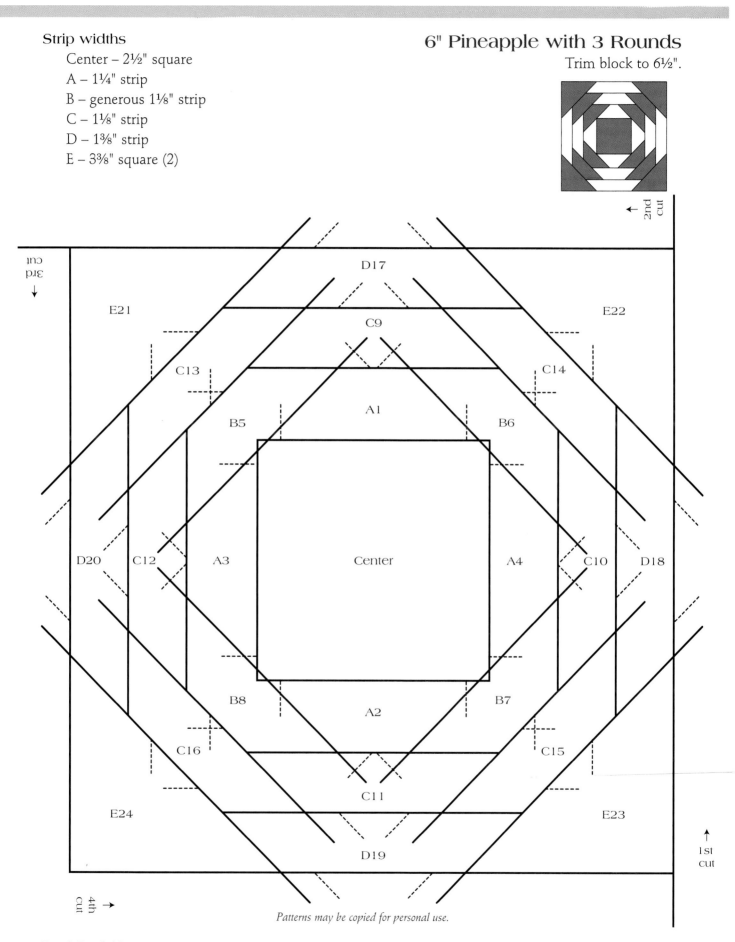

← 2nd cut

3rd cut ↓

D17

E21   E22

C9

C13   C14

A1

B5   B6

D20   C12   A3   Center   A4   C10   D18

B8   B7

A2

C16   C15

C11

E24   E23

D19

↑ 1st cut

← 4th cut

Patterns may be copied for personal use.

6" Wild Goose Chase

Trim block to 6½".

Strip widths

A – generous 1⅝" square
B – generous 1⅝" square
C – generous 2" square
D – scant 1⅛" strip
E – 1⅜" strip
F – 2⅝" square

Cut B, C, and F squares in half diagonally.

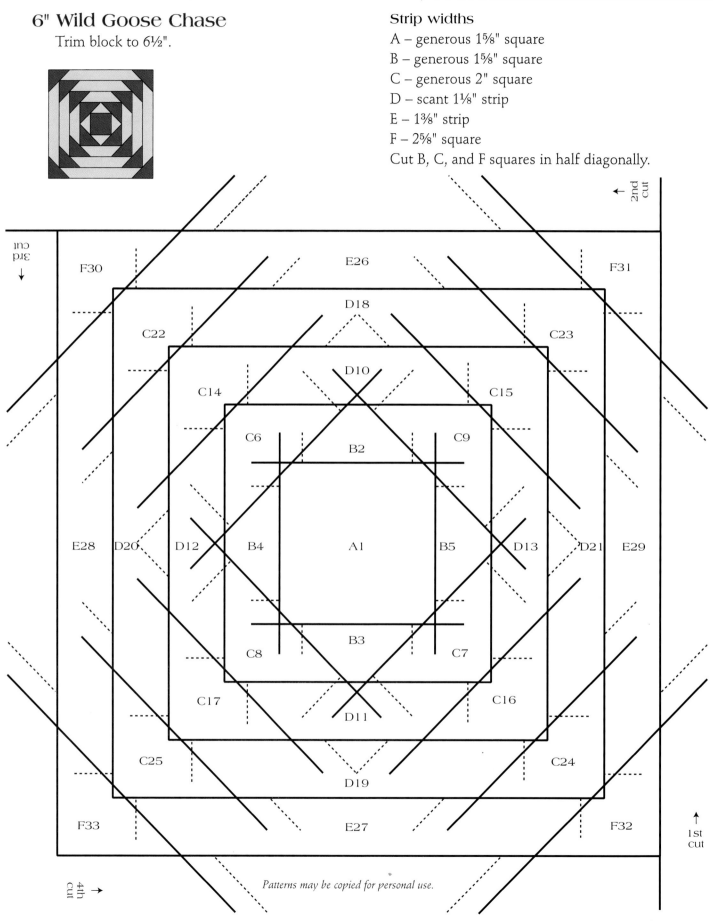

2nd cut ←

3rd cut ↓

| F30 | | E26 | | F31 |

D18

| C22 | | | | C23 |

D10

| C14 | | | | C15 |

| C6 | | | C9 |

B2

| E28 | D20 | D12 | B4 | A1 | B5 | D13 | D21 | E29 |

B3

| C8 | | | C7 |

| C17 | | | | C16 |

D11

| C25 | | | | C24 |

D19

| F33 | | E27 | | F32 |

↑ 1st cut

4th cut →

Patterns may be copied for personal use.

Beyond Barn Raising

The setting variations for the Log Cabin block are endless and offer a wide range of design possibilities. So much so, that it is often difficult to stop playing with the blocks and get back to the business of making a quilt.

The Log Cabin block can be substituted for any block that contains a half-square triangle.

MOUNTAIN RETREAT on page 56 is an example of this. For inspiration, study classic quilt blocks. If the block is made up of half-square triangles and plain squares, it can easily be adapted for a Log Cabin. With careful fabric placement, Courthouse Steps can replace a quarter-square triangle or an Hourglass block.

Blocks as Borders

Use traditional Log Cabin or Thick and Thin blocks as border designs. Notice the third illustration in the second row. The inner border was cre- ated by using a contrasting fabric in the last log in every block. A step square was used in the corner blocks to complete the border.

Piano-Key Border

A piano-key border with Off-Center corner blocks provides the perfect finish to a Log Cabin quilt. A narrow inner border between the quilt center and the strip-pieced border will solve the problem of a bulky seam allowance.

Several narrow strips sewn together are called "strata." The strips can be cut any width, usually from selvage to selvage. Staggering the placement of different fabrics will add interest and variety, making the strata less predictable.

To audition the fabrics for a piano-key border, suspend the strips over an ironing board. Plan two or more different strata with 12 strips each. A shorter stitch length will prevent the stitches from pulling out when the strata are cut into border widths.

The strips will be different lengths, so you will want to align them at one end. The other end of the strata will be ragged.

- Sew the strips together in pairs (Fig. 5–1). Do not press yet.
- Sew pairs into sets of four. Be sure to start sewing at the opposite end to help keep the strips from bowing (Fig. 5–2).
- Sew the groups of four together, again reversing the sewing direction for alternate seams.
- First press the seam as sewn. Then, with the strata right side down, place the tip of the iron next to the first seam. Pinch the next seam and gently pull until the first seam stands upright. Slide the iron along the seam to flatten it (Fig. 5–3).
- Continue pressing one seam at a time. If you are using steam, allow the strata to dry before shifting them, so they will not be distorted. Turn the strata over and press on the right side.

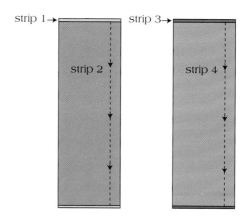

Fig. 5–1. Sew strips in pairs.

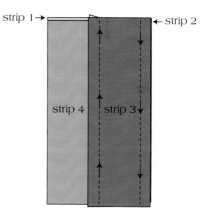

Fig. 5–2. Sew even-numbered seams one direction, odd-numbered seams the opposite direction.

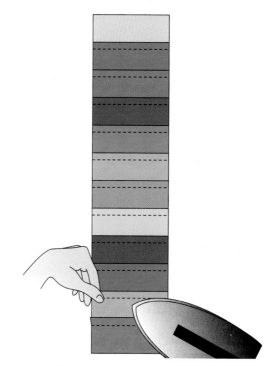

Fig. 5–3. Pull the seam allowance upright before pressing it.

- Lay the strata right side down on the cutting mat. Using two rulers and your rotary cutter, straighten the left edge of the strata.
- Cut the strata to the required border width.

Remember to include seam allowances. It will be necessary to true the edge of the strata after every second cut.

TIP: If the pieced border is too long, do not trim one of the end strips to achieve the required length. One strip that is narrower than the rest will be very noticeable. Instead, increase the seam allowances between some of the strips by a needle's width. It is not necessary to remove the original stitching lines because they are in the seam allowance.

QUILTING OPTIONS

Circular or gently flowing lines will soften the sharp lines created by the Log Cabin blocks. Single Wave can easily be adapted to fit any size square. By itself, it is very simple, but when used as an all-over design, it forms a secondary pattern, an apple core. For a completely different look, add the mirror image of Single Wave to create Pumpkin Seed quilting.

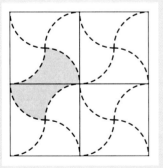

single wave

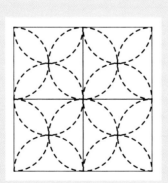

pumpkin seed

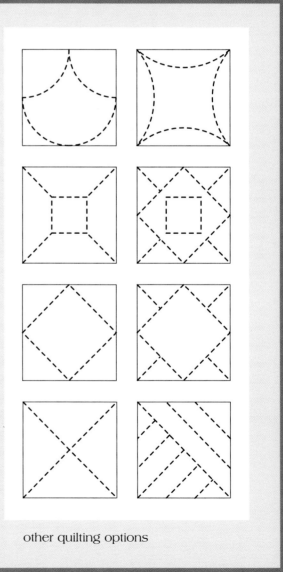

other quilting options

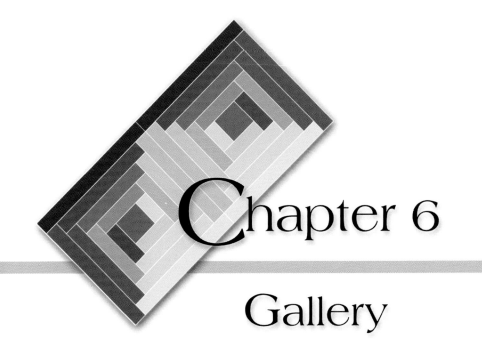

Chapter 6

Gallery

WELCOME TO MY CABIN (50" x 62"), pieced and machine quilted by the author. This quilt features a variety of 6" Log Cabin blocks set in the side of a 10" House block. A 2" sashing, 1" inner bordering, and Square-in-a-Square corner blocks complete the quilt's design.

Gallery

SPINNING IN CIRCLES (90" x 105"), pieced by Annette Blair, Helen Dupuis, Lesley Gilmour, Pat Hofmann, Mary Shore, Lilly Thorne, and Patt Wilson; machine quilted by Kirsten Yee. This quilt is a variation of one designed by Georgia Bonesteel.

TRAIL MIX (42" x 54"), pieced by Theresa Bakos, Abbotsford, B.C., Canada, and machine quilted by Carol Seeley of Campbell River, B.C., Canada.

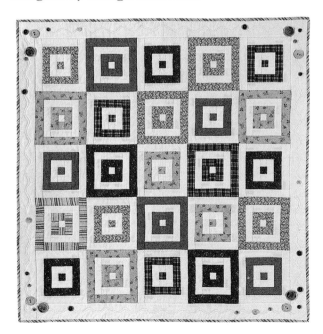

SQUARE DANCE (50" x 50"), pieced and machine quilted by Eileen Currie of Delta, B.C., Canada.

TRULY AMISH (42" x 56"), pieced, hand, and machine quilted by Betty Mensinger, White Rock, B.C., Canada.

ONE YELLOW ROSE (44" x 44"), pieced and machine quilted by Pauline Buckley of White Rock, B.C., Canada.

AWASH WITH TULIPS (56" x 73"), pieced and machine quilted by Barbara Jarvis of Fort Langley, B.C., Canada.

PLAYING WITH SQUARES (47" x 59"), pieced and machine quilted by the author.

COURTHOUSE SQUARES (38" x 46"), pieced and hand quilted by Pauline Buckley of White Rock, B.C., Canada.

GOOSE IN THE GARDEN (41½" x 41½"), pieced, hand appliquéd, and hand quilted by Helen Wadella of Surrey, B.C., Canada.

MY SUMMER CABIN (52" x 64"), pieced and machine quilted by Diane deVisser of Delta, B.C., Canada, for her daughter, Miranda.

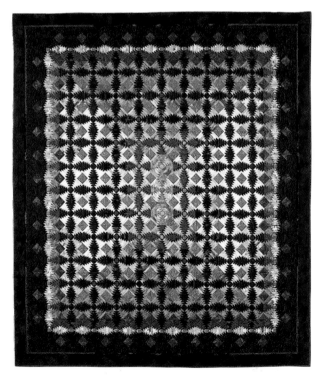

CONVERGENCE (79" x 90"), pieced and machine quilted by Val Smith of White Rock, B.C., Canada.

FLOWERS AROUND THE CABIN (63" x 63"), pieced, hand appliquéd, and hand quilted by Loraine Burchill of New Westminster, B.C., Canada. Loraine used a variation on the Cabin Posies block from *Garden Window* by Carolann M. Palmer (That Patchwork Place, 1992).

Chapter 7

Quiltmaking Tips

Here are a few of my favorite quiltmaking techniques you may find useful in your own projects.

Fitting Borders

Lay the quilt on a large flat surface and measure the quilt center and side edges from top to bottom. Measure the quilt again midway between the center and the side edges (Fig. 7–1). Record these measurements, and if the difference between the smallest and largest is minimal, choose the smallest number. If there is a large discrepancy, use the average. Divide the quilt length measurement in half.

If you have measured the quilt with a cloth tape, use the same tape to measure the border strips. The measurements on the cloth tape may differ slightly with those on your acrylic ruler. Cloth tapes stretch with age and use and should be replaced periodically.

Fold the border strip in half and lay it on a flat surface. Place the measuring tape on top. Align the half-quilt length measurement with the fabric fold. Nick the fabric at the zero end of the tape measure. Remove the tape and complete the cut with a rotary cutter. (Be sure to measure from the fold. If you mistakenly start measuring at the fabric edges, none of the pieces you end up with will be the correct length.)

Fold the quilt in half and mark the quilt center at the edge with a straight pin. Unfold the quilt and lay it on a large flat surface. Mark the center of the border edge. Place the border on top of the quilt, matching the raw edges and center marks. Pin the border strip in position, easing any extra fullness equally along the border length. Check the underside and place a pin in any seams that will lie opposite the direction of sewing. With the border on top, stitch from edge to edge with a ¼" seam allowance, backstitching at the beginning and end of the seam. Press the seam allowances toward the border. The top and bottom borders are added the same way as the side borders.

Sewing Backing Panels

Two seams equidistant from the center are preferable to one center seam (Fig. 7–2). Not only does it look more pleasing, but it is also practical. The area of most stress for a bed quilt is the quilt center. Moving the seams away from the center helps reduce wear and tear on the seams.

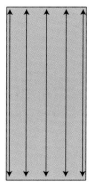

Fig. 7–1. Measure the quilt center, side edges, and midway between the center and each side edge.

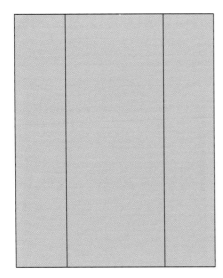

Fig. 7–2. Two seams are preferable to one seam in the center.

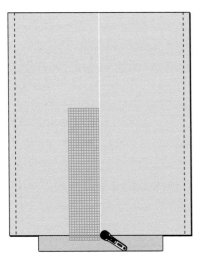

Fig. 7–3. Rotary cut through the middle of the top fabric.

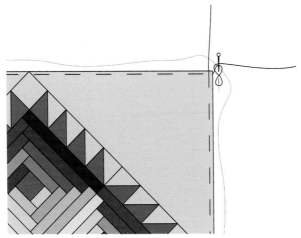

Fig. 7–4. Wrap the thread ends in a figure-8 around a straight pin in the batting.

For large bed quilts, remove the selvages and place the backing panels right sides together and sew both long edges with a ½" seam allowance, creating a tube. Place a cutting mat inside the tube and, using a rotary cutter and ruler, cut through the middle of the top fabric (Fig. 7–3). Press the seam allowances open.

Securing Machine Quilting

Log Cabin quilts can be hand or machine quilted, but because there are so many seams, most quilters choose to machine quilt. Start and end each seam with four or five very small stitches to secure the seam.

Here is a timesaving tip from professional quilter and author Maurine Noble: If your sewing machine has stitch memory, set the straight stitch on 2.75 and select the zigzag stitch. Set the width to zero and the length to .5mm. The zigzag has been changed to a very short straight stitch. With the machine still on zigzag, sew four to five small stitches. Select the straight stitch and sew the seam, stopping ⅛" from the end. Again, select the zigzag to secure the seam. By taking advantage of this feature, you only have to switch between the two programmed stitches to secure the seam rather than changing the straight-stitch length.

The first step in machine quilting is to anchor the quilt. Stitch in the ditch (sew adjacent to the seam on the side without the allowances) between all the blocks vertically and then horizontally. Once the quilt layers have been securely fastened, the majority of the safety pins can be removed. It is much easier to plan and mark the quilting design if your eye is not distracted by a lot of safety pins.

Ensuring Quilts Hang Straight

Have you ever noticed quilts on display or in magazines that have wavy or rippled edges? They don't hang straight, and the corners appear larger than the middle of the quilt. There are several explanations for this.

- The quilt top was not measured and the borders were not cut to size. Instead, border strips were laid on the quilt top, stitched in position, and the excess fabric trimmed after the border was attached.
- In many instances, the body of the quilt top was pieced and the border was not.
- The body of the quilt was quilted and the border was not quilted.
- The border may have been stretched because of excessive handling before the binding was applied.

To ensure that your quilts hang straight, cut a single strand of hand-quilting thread 12" longer than one of the quilt's sides. Baste along the edge of the quilt with stitches a generous ⅛" long and ⅛" from the quilt edge. Baste to the end of the side but do not tie off or anchor the stitches. Remove the needle and prepare the other three sides in the same way.

Lay the quilt on a large, flat surface and measure the quilt from top to bottom and side to side at the center, sides, and midway between the center and the quilt edge. Write these measurements down. If there is a big difference between the measurements, you will not be able to adjust the border length to match the quilt. The outside edges may lie flat, but the border will ripple. Gather up the extra length by pulling on the loose thread ends. Your eye and the quilt will tell you how much you need to adjust. Before securing the threads, check that both side measurements are the same, and also check the top and bottom.

If the quilt is going to be displayed, pin a temporary hanging sleeve (I have a variety of sizes just for this purpose) to the quilt back and hang the quilt on a bare wall, not a design wall. This one extra step will prevent surprises or disappointments.

To secure the gathering, wrap the threads in a figure-8 around a straight pin placed in the batting ½" beyond the quilt edge (Fig. 7–4). Distribute the gathered fabric evenly across the border. Do not leave any excess in the corners. Lay a

square ruler on the corners to ensure that they are square. You are ready to apply the binding.

Here's a little tip for turning a corner with binding. Sew to within 2" of the corner. With the binding strip positioned on the edge, align the ¼" line of a clear acrylic 1" x 6" ruler on the quilt edge closest to you. Place a straight pin in the binding at the ruler's edge to tell you exactly where to stop stitching (Fig. 7–5). Remove the ruler. Sew as close as possible to the pin without hitting or going past it. It may be necessary to decrease the stitch length to accomplish this.

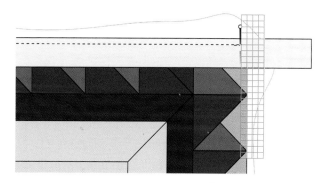

Fig. 7–5. Place a pin in the binding at the ruler's edge.

Making a Label

The perfect label for a Log Cabin quilt can be made with fabric strips left over from the quilt top. For example, you can trace a 7" Log Cabin block with four rounds, omitting the center square and the first and second round of logs. Cut a 4½" square of light-colored fabric for the center and complete the block in the normal way.

Consider attaching the label before turning the binding to the back of the quilt. Not only does it save time, it looks neater. In addition, the label becomes part of the quiltmaking process, not an add-on when the quilt is finished. Press the top and right side edges of the label under ¼". Align the left side and bottom edges with the quilt edges and pin or baste in position. Turn the binding as you normally would and secure the label to the quilt back with a hand blind stitch.

Bibliography

Encyclopedia of Pieced Quilt Patterns, compiled by Barbara Brackman. American Quilter's Society, Paducah, Kentucky, 1993.

Easy Does It Quilts, Georgia Bonesteel. Oxmoor House, Birmingham, Alabama, 1995.

A Log Cabin Notebook, Mary Ellen Hopkins. ME Publications, Cardiff by the Sea, California, 1991.

Corners in the Cabin, Paulette Peters. That Patchwork Place, Bothel, Washington, 1992.

Log Cabins – New Techniques for Traditional Quilts, Janet Kime. Cutting Edge Quilt Designs, Inc., Edmonds, Washington, 1992.

The Critter Quilt, Brandywine Designs, P.O. Box 135, Chanhassen, Minnesota, 1997.

Machine Quilting Made Easy!, Maurine Noble. That Patchwork Place, Bothel, Washington, 1994.

Block Party, Marsha McCloskey. Rodale Press, Emmaus, Pennsylvania, 1998.

Resources

The Electric Quilt Company
Owned by Dean and Penny McMorris
419 Gould Street, Suite 2
Bowling Green, OH 43402
   Computer quilt design programs

Visit the author's website for new designs and workdate updates:
   www.brendabrayfield.com

Teacher's Guide

A Log Cabin workshop is a popular class for quilt shops and guilds. Everyone loves a Log Cabin!

Lesson Plan 1
LOG CABIN – EXPLORE THE POSSIBILITIES

PREREQUISITE: Rotary cutting skills, before cutting is required in class.

DURATION: Two three-hour sessions with two weeks between classes.

PROJECT: Thirty-six 6" Log Cabin blocks with three rounds.

CLASS 1: Students learn basic block construction, trimming, and assembly. For homework, students complete 36 blocks.

CLASS 2: Students explore the endless design possibilities of the Log Cabin block. Use the design sets on page 115 as a guide. Suggest they bring a camera to this class.

Lesson Plan 2
INTRODUCTION TO TOP FOUNDATION PIECING

PREREQUISITE: Rotary cutting skills, before cutting is required in class.

DURATION: Two three-hour sessions.

PROJECT: Tulip Bouquet Table Runner (page 39), comprised of 12 – 6" Log Cabin blocks with three rounds and four 6" Single Tulip blocks.

CLASS 1: Students learn basic block construction, trimming, and assembly.

CLASS 2: Show samples and explain construction of Courthouse Steps, Triangles in the Corner, Off-Center, Thick and Thin, Snail's Trail, and Pineapple Blocks. Students work on Single Tulip and Square-in-a-Square. Suggestion: If you start with a light-colored 3½" square for the Square-in-a-Square block, students can use it as a quilt label.

Lesson Plan 3
LOG CABIN SAMPLER

PREREQUISITE: Rotary cutting skills. Cutting is done before first class.

DURATION: Two three-hour sessions.

PROJECT: In this class, students learn a variety of blocks. Strips and squares should be pre-cut and labeled before class.

Suggested blocks include Log Cabin, Courthouse Steps, Off-Center, Thick and Thin, Triangles in the Corner, Single Tulip, Snail's Trail, Square-in-a-Square, Simple Pineapple, and Wild Goose Chase. A third class could be added to include setting the blocks, making borders, and binding edges.

CLASS 1: Students learn basic block construction and trimming as they work on Log Cabin, Steps to the Cabin, and Triangles in the Corner. Courthouse Steps, Off-Center, Around the World, and Thick and Thin can be demonstrated and completed for homework.

CLASS 2: Variations on the Log Cabin block are introduced as the students learn to construct blocks with triangles and angled logs. Suggested blocks: Single Tulip, Square-in-a-Square, Snail's Trail, Wild Goose Chase, and Pineapple blocks.

Other AQS Books

This is only a small selection of the books available from the American Quilter's Society. AQS books are known worldwide for timely topics, clear writing, beautiful color photos, and accurate illustrations and patterns. The following books are available from your local bookseller, quilt shop, or public library.

Linda Franz
Quilted Diamonds
Jane Austen, Jane Stickle & Friends

#5847   US$24.95

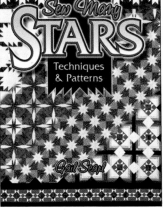

Sew Many **STARS** Techniques & Patterns
Gail Searl

#5176   US$24.95

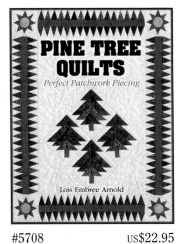

PINE TREE QUILTS
Perfect Patchwork Piecing
Lois Embree Arnold

#5708   US$22.95

Pineapple Quilts
New Quilts from an Old Favorite

#5898   US$16.95

Stellar JOURNEYS
Flying Geese & Star Quilts

#5852   US$19.95

BETHANY S. REYNOLDS
Stack-n-Whackier QUILTS
ANOTHER Magic Stack-n-Whack BOOK

#5850   US$21.95

FIRM FOUNDATIONS
TECHNIQUES AND QUILT BLOCKS FOR PRECISION PIECING
JANE HALL AND DIXIE HAYWOOD

#4594   US$18.95

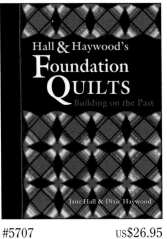

Hall & Haywood's
Foundation QUILTS
Building on the Past
Jane Hall & Dixie Haywood

#5707   US$26.95

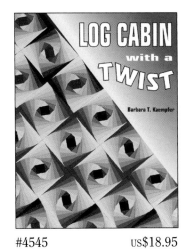

LOG CABIN with a TWIST
Barbara T. Kaempfer

#4545   US$18.95

Look for these books nationally or call **1-800-626-5420**